THE FRONTIERS OF KNOWLEDGE

JUDITH STIEHM, EDITOR
Published by the
University of Southern California Press
September 1976

Manufactured in the United States of America
Library of Congress Catalog Card Number
ISBN 0-88474-036-6

To the young women and men who will explore frontiers still unimagined.

This volume was made possible by men like Milton Kloetzel and Donald Lewis, who contributed institutional money, and by the women of the University of Southern California Chapter, 1974-75, of Mortar Board—Diana Gerhardt, Amy Gunderson, and Barbara MacEachern—who gave inspiration, energy, and wisdom to its preparation and completion.

CONTENTS

THE FRONTIERS OF KNOWLEDGE

JUDITH STIEHM

University of Southern California

THOSE WHO PRESS beyond the known, who cross the frontier between familiar and new knowledge, are of a special sort. Sometimes they are private people whose explorations never attract public notice; sometimes their zest and curiosity are communicated as openly and freely as are measles. In this volume six explorers describe their intellectual development and their current investigations in a way that moves us to follow their lead.

Doing so might be made easier if one could perceive what is common to the lives and works of the accomplished. Only one thing seems certain: great industry underpins the work of the most talented and trained thinkers and doers. Great variety is the rule when it comes to background, environment, styles, and rewards. Indeed, one is never quite confident that society even recognizes her most singular members. Prizes, chairs, and contracts may be richly deserved by those who win them. Those whose lot is anonymity, unemployment, or a security check may also deserve what they receive. Somehow, one feels less sure about the latter.

In reviewing available biographies and autobiographies of recognized and rewarded scholars, one finds few narratives which deal with the intellectual development of women. In the best accounts of the process of discovery, whether they be in James D. Watson's *The Double Helix*, Davis' *Oppenheimer and Lawrence*, or any of Arthur Koestler's studies of the acquisition of knowledge, the roles played by women are meager. If one assumes that raw (genetic) talent is indiscriminately allocated between men and women, one becomes curious to know why there is such a sexually selective realization of talent.

First, one must assume that endowment is not enough. Talent must be trained. Talent can be developed in isolation or can be self-developed in only a few fields, principally those devoted to self-expression. Here there are and have always been examples of high female achievement. These include Emily Dickinson and Maya Angelou in poetry, Ella Fitzgerald and Joan Baez in voice, and Louise Nevelson and June Wayne in painting. Unfortunately, training is not as readily available to young women as it is to young men. Further, it is not usually something that one acquires or fails to acquire by oneself. By definition, training requires investment and discipline. Both or either may be provided by a closely knit, success-oriented family; alternatively they may be provided by a society which has high expectations for individuals of particular classes and of a particular gender. Again, training requires an investment of money and of time and of attention. All call for exceptional self- and/or social discipline.

Let us briefly examine the subtle ways society disciplines men rather than women to achieve. For years we have known that both families and scholastic gatekeepers have doubted the value of investing in expensive, specialized training for women. Their grounds were that women failed to "use" their education once they became involved in marriage and in having a family. Now, of course, we know that there are a number of factors which relate to whether or not a woman works. One is that society regularly fails to reward trained working women in the same way that it rewards men. A brutal demonstration of this is the finding of the U.S. Department of Labor that women with a college degree earn as much as black men with a high school degree or as white men with an eighth-grade education. At the same time, however, we also know that, even though poorly rewarded, women with professional and graduate degrees usually *do* use them. In other words, one part of the problem may be that women aren't getting enough or the right kind of education, not that they are getting "too much." A second part is that they are not rewarded for the education they do acquire.

FAMILIAL INVESTMENTS IN CHILDREN

A vivid example of the different ways families seem to invest in their children can be seen in the studies of Margaret Henning. In her study of top female business executives, Dr. Henning found that, *without exception,* each was an only child *or* the eldest of all-female siblings. In short, each was raised in a family which had no sons. This, of course, has interesting implications for a society approaching zero population growth. If more and more families contain only a few children, more and more of them will be "son-less," and more and more young women may receive the kind of familial investment required to achieve high success.

Regardless of parental attitude, some children are expected by society to achieve (even to achieve brilliantly), and pressures are built into their everyday training. To illustrate, even the most "liberated" women usually speak of a goal limited to independence or self-sufficiency. This reminds one of the teenager's perception of adulthood as an age of individualistic voluntary behavior. What we elders know is that, at least for the middle and upper classes, adulthood does not really mean independence; it means *having* dependents. The adult male is socialized to expect not only to have to support himself, but also to have to support a wife, children, and possibly his parents. The pressures of this kind of expectation seem to make men of all ages far more serious about themselves than are women. Another homespun example might be helpful. Who takes music lessons? Who plays in the elementary school orchestra/band? In the senior high school? In college? In the Los Angeles Philharmonic? The answer seems to be here, as in many other fields, that, while more females may learn some music, it is males who stick with it. It is men in whom time and money are invested, and it is they who finally profit from or realize a return on that investment.

A few women (and precise numbers are available for most fields) do receive the same training as the most successful men in their field. Even if we assume that part of the reason for women's low representation in elite training institutions is their own "lack of motivation," we must nevertheless examine other factors. To begin, performance is not the only criterion for admission to the best institutions. If it were, all admissions could be done by a computer on the basis of grades and test scores. However, consideration is also given to where one has been, where one wants to go, and where one can be expected to arrive. "Where one has been" means that preparation at certain schools is given added weight; that this is unfair to some males who lack equal access to these usually private and expensive educational institutions is taken into account by special recruitment of and programs for "disadvantaged" students. The fact that many of "the best" preparatory schools and colleges legally discriminate against even "advantaged women" (some by remaining all-male, some by having a quota for women) is often forgotten. The result, of course, is that the pool of most-eligible men is larger than the pool of most-eligible women. Using sex-segregated schooling to prepare more trained men than women occurs most often in the Northeast, but this phenomenon extends also to religious schools (many of them Catholic) where sex-segregated education is by no means extinct. There, again, more opportunities are offered to men than to women, and there, too, regardless of the total schooled, opportunities are *not* equal.

SOME INTERESTING IRONIES

This unequal situation yields several interesting ironies. First, many men from the best training institutions now direct much of our nation's business. Many of these men never trained with women. They prepped at all-male schools, attended all-male undergraduate colleges, attended nearly all-male professional and graduate schools and (those fifty and over) served in a mostly male military. They would have little reason to believe, given their experience, that women could be their equals. Today, however, most top educational institutions are undergoing controlled integration. Limited numbers of very superior women are gaining admission to previously all-male institutions. The result is that the leaders now being trained are not only having the experience of being trained with women, they are frequently being trained with women *superior* to themselves! In the future, it will be interesting to see how this affects their attitudes toward female leadership. A second irony lies in numerous findings that women from sex-segregated schools actually achieve more in later life than do women from sex-integrated schools—even though their total opportunities are fewer and even though the "sisters" in a paired set of single-sex schools (such as Barnard and Columbia) are often thought to be less intellectually demanding.

Accomplishment in training institutions involves meeting specified standards through individual effort, that is, intellectual virtuoso activity. In the work world, however, any specialist works within an intricately subdivided and complex social system. Work is accomplished not by soloists but by a team. (Often individual actors are, or act as though they are, unaware of this.) This is the third and perhaps the most fascinating prerequisite for intellectual achievement: that one be a part of the complex social structure which facilitates excellent work. To be outside of it is to be severely handicapped.

Again, in admitting people to training, criteria said to predict future contributions are sometimes used. Often this is represented as an attempt to assess motivation or "seriousness." However, sometimes it is charged that this involves the selecting of people like oneself: the perpetuation of one's own image. It may also involve an unconscious estimate of how the individual is going to be accepted by the team, how the social structure of the discipline will or will not accommodate the individual. In each of these cases, women could expect to be, and have been, underselected.

The social ground and personal milieu of intellectual achievement has long been the object of study. Sometimes designated the "sociology of knowledge," this field has been enriched by the work of social historians like Arnold Hauser, scientific historians like Thomas Kuhn, and autobiographers like James D. Watson, John Stuart Mill, and Margaret Mead. From this body of work it seems clear that both men and women have severely underestimated a woman's intellectual disadvantage of not being "one of the boys."

Virginia Woolf's *A Room of One's Own* elegantly delineates the problems of an intellectual woman. Although her art was one capable of solo execution and even though she was well integrated into a thriving literary circle, Woolf understood the devastation separate development brings to most women who are serious about their work. Her description of the agitated Beadle keeping women on the gravel path, of women gently being kept out of Oxbridge libraries, of sole, partridge, and confections at the men's college and beef, custard, and prunes at the women's are symbols of more severe deprivations. In a vivid fantasy, Woolf demonstrates the penalties society exacts by portraying the sad fate of an imaginary, gifted sister of William Shakespeare named Judith. Indeed, she even proposes that society does have historical evidence of past female genius; this, she argues, includes works done by "Anon.," the tragic madness and self-destruction of numerous women, the practice of witchcraft, and the extraordinary mothering of extraordinary men.

THE EVOLUTION OF A MASTERPIECE

"Masterpieces are not single and solitary births; they are the outcome of many years of thinking in common, of thinking by the body of the people, so that the experience of the mass is behind the single voice," Woolf says, and many social scientists would agree. This means that women's lack of experience, intercourse, and travel limit them. Even George Eliot, who defied convention by living with a married man, among other things, mostly worked in seclusion. Only a few uncommon women have felt free to even endeavor things essayed by very ordinary men, and only a handful of those have gained their experience purposefully and through their own initiative. Even today too many "self-defining" women are actually defining themselves defiantly or compliantly. They do not behave confidently or unself-consciously.

Success which "prompts to exertion" and habit "which facilitates success" are omitted from the usual female experience. Yet, Woolf concludes, "to be a man or woman pure and simple" is fatal, for one's work ceases "to be fertilized." This seems to be the secret of the success of the women authors in this collection: they have not denied their sex but they have also had the capacity to move beyond it. They are themselves, and they think of reality in a sex-transcending manner.

The purpose of these autobiographical essays is to convey how each of six gifted and trained individuals came to her profession, how her work is conducted, and where the current boundaries lie in her field. Their benefit is, first, that they provide pleasure; second, that they give inspiration (and there can be no doubt of that, given the enthusiasm of the audiences privileged to hear the oral presentations on which these essays are based); and third, that they instruct, that their experiences with their various intellectual networks show how they have been both a part of and also apart from those networks. Like Mannheim's "mobile men," women may have a special insight into their society because even the most achieving of them has had a special relationship to her subject.

The first piece is by the indefatigable conductor Antonia Brico. No one can doubt that Maestro Brico can create only with great social cooperation. As a conductor, she must inspire and direct the efforts of the trained and talented members of an orchestra; yet she must first be invited to direct by an orchestra board concerned with finance, as well as music, and the public must accept her and support her by purchasing tickets or she will not be allowed to exercise her talent. Although this grand woman demonstrated rare talent, persisted through the most excellent training, and was showcased as a female novelty in the launching of her career, she was not able to gain the cooperation of an employer—a board that found no fault with either her musical ability or her capacity to draw an audience as a conductor. Brico argued that sex is no impediment for musicians and for music lovers, but to little avail. To perform, she was forced to create her own instrument—to found her own orchestra—and she did.

The most recent highlight of Brico's career was her venture into a new medium, film. In *Antonia: Portrait of The Woman,* her musicianship and vitality were carried to a broad audience. She has again been offered a round of guest opportunities—a well-deserved honor—but it should be noted that these are honors, one shot invitations. She has not been offered institutional support. Inertia is still not on her side. Performance, more or less success, has had no chance to become routine.

Cynthia Epstein, a student of women's role in the contemporary world describes a quite different experience, one in which her talents *were* recognized. She was selected by examination for special academic schooling when still in grade school and was treated as intellectually serious in a small, co-ed liberal arts college. Her talent was overlooked only when she entered and then left a male-dominated law school. She was fortunate enough later on to find colleagues and a sponsor (indeed, a co-author) in the field she chose for graduate work. Further, sociology is a field into which women are integrated and it is one in which she has won great distinction. Her wry description of her growth reminds us of how unconsciously most of us choose, and of the influence serendipity (social institutions) appears to have on our choices.

Chance affected the career even of electrical engineer Mildred Dresselhaus. What if the Fulbright Program had not materialized during her senior year? What if she had not gained entry to Hunter High School through her mastery of the violin? Still, her account reflects the spare, directed, organized nature of her mind and work. Precision and impersonality dominate her serious work and lucidity her every statement. Yet she, too, made choices based on roles women play, on her marriage, and on her motherhood. She also notes that there are some advantages to having a bigger handicap than one's sex (such as poverty, which teaches survival) and that being an "only" or unique woman (rather than being part of a minority) can be helpful. Still her spirit sounds like that of Brico—"there is no such thing as impossible," "I know there is nothing I cannot do."

With joy and poetry, Celeste Ulrich celebrates her study of movement. Her decision to devote her life to physical education was not easy; her convictions were questioned (1) because she was female and (2) because she was bright. Nevertheless, the integration of Ulrich's life and work, of her mind and body, of her strength and beauty, are all on display in this essay. The protection she was afforded by a profession (women's physical education teacher) *and* a school reserved only for women are worth noting.

Anthropologist Laura Nader describes the development of a mind which is integrated rather than departmentalized. It took a letter from an older brother to tell her what she was, and a special act by her college president to name the B.A. she had earned, but the fact that "names" were hard to come by is perhaps the best proof that Nader's work is pioneering.

Rooted in the happenings and events around her as much as in the codes and concerns of her discipline, Nader has consistently succeeded both with and without the support of colleagues and grant reviewers. Feeling "different" may have made her more sensitive than most to the exercise of power—particularly to that kind of unaccountable, irresponsible, institutional power that touches the lives of most of us.

Why? Who made that decision? What were the women doing? Florence Howe suggests that these questions are critical to feminist scholarship. She provides some answers to these queries as she outlines the stages of her own and of women's education in this country. Like Nader, Howe understands that power affects knowledge just as knowledge creates power. Howe neglects neither aspect as she points out that strong arguments are still made for a special, appropriate education for women, as well as for an equal and similar education to that of men. Nevertheless, Howe, who demonstrates that possession of a Ph.D. is incidental to inquiry, argues that the question of knowledge must be examined anew and that power must be used if only to turn society's procession "half an inch off course."

ONE UNDEFLECTED STEP AT A TIME

ANTONIA BRICO

Denver, Colorado

GOOD AFTERNOON, LADIES and Gentlemen. I am not a lecturer. We'll start that way. I just ramble, I ramble and I talk about whatever I feel like, and I have enough information inside myself that I can ramble. Right now I'm mad, not at you, but I've just come from a newspaper interview, never mind for what newspaper, but the interview has made me angry and perhaps my anger can generate some thinking by you. Now anytime you'd like to interrupt me, anytime you'd like to ask a question do so, but let me try to tell you something about my life.

When I was interviewed just now it was by someone who brought out all the negative aspects of my life. I'll tell you about it, but I want you to know that I am an optimist from the word go. If I had not been an optimist, I would not yet, even after years and years of frustration and work, be conducting or hoping to conduct the major orchestras in this country.

I don't know how many of you know anything about the movie, *Antonia, Portrait of the Woman,* or anything about my past but if I had not been an optimist I would have been dead long ago, and I'm going to start with what I thought would be the conclusion. You'll have to excuse me, I am going to start there because of this interview and say, "Young people, do not, I reiterate, do *not* let yourself be deflected from what you want to do."

To teachers and to parents I say, "Do not try, and I emphasize this, do *not* try to make decisions for your children." To teachers especially, do not ever say to a student, "Oh, but you won't make a success at this so there is no use even trying." That's what they said to me years and years, never mind how many years, ago, and while it did not stop me it hurt me. In retrospect I can see that this interviewer who so agitated me brought back

those feelings. You know that when you have sad feelings that you have
repressed, about an unhappiness or sadness, or a death, or something that
went quite wrong, you repress those feelings, don't you? Nod, yes, yes,
yes. All right, now what this interviewer did (he didn't mean to, certainly)
was to succeed in bringing out all the negative and sad aspects of what has
happened to me, all the hurts, all the disappointments, all the frustrations,
and now I am letting these feelings out on you. Instead of talking positively and that's what I want you to do, ladies and gentlemen, students—
think positive!—what he did was *not* to say, aren't you thrilled to death that
because of the love, devotion, ingenuity, knowhow, and money of one
Judy Collins (I think the film did not say that she was a piano student of
mine for years and that I got her to the point where she played the
Rachmaninov Concerto before she went off in a different direction, and
she certainly did very well for herself in that direction!), instead of saying,
positively, "Isn't it wonderful that thanks to this film and to Judy Collins I
now have concerts I never thought I would ever have?", he said, "Don't
you regret your wasted years?"

You must know that for years and years I (and other women) labored
under the prejudices of managers and boards of directors. We did *not*
suffer, and let me reiterate that, from the prejudices of the orchestras.
Sometimes people say orchestras don't want to play with women. Don't
they? Orchestras are composed of musicians. How many musicians are in
this hall? Raise your hands. Good. Orchestras don't care who is at the
helm. They don't care whether it's a he or a she or an it or a that, or what
color or what religion or what background; they just don't care. All musicians care about is whether the he or the she on the podium, the person
who moves this little magic wand about, knows or doesn't know what he
or she is talking about. That's all musicians care. This is why I remain an
incredible optimist and have been since the word go. If I had not been I
would never have started this bloody business of trying to be a conductor;
and don't anyone ever describe Brico as a "woman conductor;" that's
enough to make me jump down your throat. I am *a* conductor, period. So,
again, instead of stressing the positive effects of the film, this interviewer
kept asking, "Doesn't it bother you that it is because of the film and not
because of your ability that you now have more concerts than ever before?" You see, he was trying to stress the negative instead of emphasizing
the positive. I did say that I well realize this should have happened ten,
fifteen, twenty years ago. But, I also said, "I am grateful for what has
happened." Then he insisted, "But isn't it really terrible, isn't it tragic that
it didn't happen ten or fifteen years ago? Can you really enjoy it now?"
Well, I must say that I am deliriously happy! But there he was—a negativ-
ist—a man who didn't want me to be deliriously happy! A man who
wanted me to be utterly miserable over what I did not have instead of enjoying what I *do* have.

'ALL IN THE WORLD I CARE ABOUT'

Now, what sense is that? What good does it do to cry over a past that didn't happen? You understand what I mean? I think life is great, don't you? I'm going to conduct your Hollywood Bowl. I think that's marvelous. And what did he say? He said, "Instead of being glad about that, aren't you sad, don't you think it's too bad that you're not conducting the Los Angeles Philharmonic at the Music Center?" Oh, this went on and on and on ... I wouldn't bother you with this except it made me fighting mad. You see that's the whole trouble, that's the reason in a sense that we have wars, because people look at the bad, not the good. Now I am not a Pollyanna, not by any means. I've suffered, but I do think that when you get something great happening to you what do you care whether it's in the Hollywood Bowl or a Los Angeles auditorium? I have said to Judith and I have said in a thousand interviews, literally a thousand interviews, "I love to conduct, and that's all in the world I care about." How it comes, with what orchestra I could care less.

When I was a student at the University of Berlin I conducted the Berlin Philharmonic in my world debut. It was terrible to conduct the best first. You see, as my professors said, "It really doesn't prove anything much—you must go out to the sticks and conduct little orchestras and little bands filled with people who don't know much, with people who need you to train them; the Berlin Philharmonic can play practically by itself." Well, that is just what I did. I was in a position to conduct in Poland, in Warsaw, in Lodz, in Poznan, in Villna, and in a number of other small places. Oh, I was conducting then! I was tickled to death! The orchestras weren't great shakes but *I was conducting.* I'm very, very consistent on that one point; on others I may vary, but on that one point I am logical and consistent: all I wanted to do and all I want to do is to conduct. I don't care whether it's an army band in Monterey, California (which I have conducted), or an inferior orchestra in Poland. One forgets all about whether people are washed, unwashed, or what—one simply conducts. When I conducted in Latvia, and I'm sure this never happened to a male conductor, I conducted Berlioz, a Hungarian dance. Now this thing gives the trombones a great big solo at the end, and when I was through they applauded and applauded and applauded. Then I went backstage and then quickly came out to take the bows real fast before the applause stopped (you know how that is), and just as I was going back on stage this great big Russian with a Russian embroidered shirt and long hair grabbed me and hugged me and swung me around three or four times, and I thought what for, what for, what for? And you know why? Because there's that part at the end where the trombones go ba ba ba ba ba da da da da da da da ... and he said all the conductors do it too fast and you *didn't!* You did it so I had a chance to really play it!

Now what I'm trying to tell you is I have always had one central idea, and this creature today was trying to make me unhappy. But he did not succeed. He just made me mad. He said isn't it tragic? And I said, "I'm conducting, I'm conducting, I'm conducting! What difference does it make whether it's here or there, or what I'm conducting or whether it's more than I did before or less?" The big thing, the big issue, what you must remember is, "Do not be deflected."

Do not care what anybody says. When I was young and foolish and seventeen and wanted to be a conductor it was, of course, even worse than it is now, and the professor I loved the most in all the world said to me, "It won't work, Antonia, it won't work. Even if you get accepted into schools it won't work. Nobody wants a woman conductor." How's that for your ego? Pretty bad, right? Well, it just went in one ear and out the other. I replied, "I want to conduct."

Other people at the University of California, Berkeley, got violently angry with me. One said, "Antonia, don't be stupid! Here I can get you a nice position, a nice safe position with tenure and this and that right here at Berkeley. Don't try this other nonsense, it's ridiculous." I said, "Will you give me a letter of introduction to the greatest conductor alive to-day?"(That was Dr. Karl Muck in Boston.) This man, who played trombone in his orchestra said, "Yes, I'll give you an introduction." Then in New York I had a piano master named Sigismond Stojowski—a marvelous pianist—who said, "Antonia, don't you do it. You're going to get heartbroken." I said, "Will you give me an introductory letter to Dr. Karl Muck?" (Dr. Karl Muck had conducted Mr. Stojowski's piano concerto with Paderewski playing the solo.) He said, "Yes, Antonia, yes, Antonia."

You see I just never listened to those who tried to discourage me. But you have to be very strong. You know, once there was an article about me in the San Francisco newspaper and the headline called me—isn't that awful?—the stubborn Dutchman. It's true. I was born in Holland, of Dutch and Italian parents. There couldn't be anything worse than that combination. That's because the Italian says, "I want to be a conductor," and the Dutch says, "Be practical." But then I finally managed to get the two of us Bricos together and we decided we were going to channel all the Dutch stubbornness into being a conductor. I thought then—I was so optimistic!—that if I did a good job at everything that's all that would be necessary. Of course I found out differently. It wasn't all that was necessary. You see, I was born in the wrong body. The manager of the New York Philharmonic explained it this way, "Brico, 75 percent of the audiences on Friday afternoons at the Philharmonic are women, and they want to see a male conductor." What kind of nonsense is that?

Well, anyway I plowed on and I plowed ahead but now I still have to go back, back to the beginning. When I was ten years old my foster mother took me to a band concert in Oakland. The first thing I thought was what a marvelous thing that a little bitty stick like that can make so many people play together so marvelously. I was real childlike. I just kept thinking how can that one little stick do all that? And that, you see, was the germ.

'IF PEOPLE AND TEACHERS ONLY KNEW'

Now I'm supposed to talk about influences on my life. Influences are enormously important; if people and teachers only knew how much they influence young people they might think a little more before they speak. If you casually toss a thought into the air it can be very dangerous. You can say things you don't mean and things which have all kinds of waves and repercussions. So, if you toss good thoughts into the air that is a marvelous thing, and when teachers are interested in a student that can do wonders for that student. Now I have had great influences and I have also had a philosophy which says, "If the first step is successful, that is an indication that you should go on, and if the second step is successful you should go on to the third." I felt true inspiration from Paul Steindorff. I studied with him at the University of California and he, too, said, "No, no, no, you don't want to be a conductor, you only do that because you love me." Well, all I said was, "I want to be a conductor," and so he at least went so far as to let me play the piano for his chorus rehearsals; he also let me coach singers when he did big things like the *Verdi Requiem* or Mozart's *Marriage of Figaro*. He let me do all that, and so I said to myself, "Well, if I were not meant to be a conductor then he would not have given me the chance to be his musical assistant and musical coach." You see, he gave me the belief I should take the next step. The greatest moment in my life was probably when I saw my name on the program as "musical assistant" because then I said, "Now I'm ready for the next step."

If you really want to know what can happen—if you're tough and Dutch—let me tell you another little story. You know who Paderewski was, don't you? You're not that disgustingly young. Paderewski, or Paderooski as they used to call him, was one of the world's great pianists. Well, I had to work my way through college. How many have seen the film and remember at the end where I play jazz? You know why that was? It was because I earned my way through college that way because I was politely told to leave home. You see, it's always been the opposite with me. Most people have parents who want them to go to school, want them to get an education. My foster parents didn't because they said it's no use, you'll just go and be a nice little saleswoman in a 15¢ store (in those days Woolworth's top price was 15¢) or you'll go and be a secretary. So I sneaked away to register at the University of California, and that did it. That was the end. I was out. But my foster parents didn't reckon with my Dutch blood and the fact was that when I wanted something I got it. Well, while I was in school I was also an usher in a San Francisco auditorium, a ghastly place like an arena and the first row is longer than this first row by far.

Well, I was an usher so I knew all of the rows and the numbers on every seat, so when Paderewski came for a concert I said to myself I am not going to usher for that concert, I'm going to buy a ticket! A ticket then was $5.00—that was enormous at a time when steak was 10¢ a pound. So, because I was living in Berkeley and going to school I asked a friend of mine to buy me a seat in the front row in the auditorium. She did, and mailed it to me. Well, it was in the front row, but it was the last seat way at the end of the front row. I was absolutely paralyzed with fear. I thought I can't see him! I might as well have ushered! So my head started working and it found a solution. I bought a camp stool. My friend said, "What are you going to do with a camp stool?" I said, "Wait and see!" Well, I went to the San Francisco auditorium and went directly to the center aisle and I sat my camp stool up there and pulled out a whole bunch of music. Since I knew all the ushers they didn't do anything to me, even though I was just sitting right where the piano was. Well, the ladies there were, of course, very high class people and the lady next to me had a lorgnette and she leaned over and said, "Oh, is that the way they do it in New York?" I said, "I don't know, lady, but that's the way they're doing it in San Francisco right now." Well, I sat and waited and prayed and at last Paderewski came. He made a low bow, like this, and he must have thought what's that doing out there? Still he didn't say anything and so I blissfully relaxed and had a marvelous time. Now there is a sequel to this. I wouldn't come so far to tell just a funny story if I didn't have a sequel. A few weeks later it was announced that the great pianist Sigismond Stojowski from New York would be there for summer master classes for six weeks. Of course, I couldn't afford those—they were $200 or $300—and so I brooded and thought, How dreadful, here you want to be a great musician, a great pianist, a great conductor and you can't even afford to study when somebody comes to San Francisco. Well, there seemed to be nothing I could do about it.

Now Sigismond Stojowski was a great friend of Paderewski and I, who had everything backwards, like, you know, most people want to go home and love vacations and Saturdays and Sundays, well, I hated them. I hated them with a vengeance and had ever since I was in grammar school, because all my friends' parents were on the faculty, and I was a very poor girl who wasn't dressed nicely. In fact, I knew someone very important on the faculty who was a friend of Sigismond so she said, "Antonia, how would you like to go to a reception for Stojowski?" and so I went. Well, I was introduced to him. Now, actually I had a lot of complexes because when you're told all your life that you're in the wrong body for something, you get complexes. Besides, the Dutch part of me was saying, go ahead, forge ahead, while the Italian part was sort of unnerved by people who said, "You'll never make it." So I was introduced to Stojowski and do you know what he said? He said, "Is this the girl with the camp stool?" Of course I blushed crimson and said, "I'm afraid so," and he replied, "Well, anyone who wants to hear Paderewski that badly deserves a scholarship." So the moral of that story is—don't you see that I'm consistent?— *"Don't be deflected."*

Well, I got the scholarship, and I was blissful; then Stojowski said in a weak moment, "If you come to New York I will give you a scholarship." Of course, he forgot all about it, but I didn't. I worked and worked. I did everything. I played for dances, I waited tables, I worked in the 15¢ store. I taught lessons for 50¢ and $1.00 an hour, and I worked myself right to New York. Stojowski was astonished when I wrote and said I was coming, probably he had forgotten all about it. But here again I'm consistent. I said to myself, "This step wouldn't have happened if you weren't meant to go on." Are you getting the point? When I got to New York Stojowski didn't want me to think about conducting either: "You just be satisfied, you just be a pianist, you be an accompanist, play on the radio, and so on." Well, I sneaked out and went to the Masters and Arts Institute; I think that was the precursor of the Juilliard School of Music. I went there and took a conducting class they were offering.

WHERE CONDUCTING STARTS

Now somebody asked me the other day, "Don't you have to learn all the instruments of the orchestra if you want to conduct?" Of course you do. In Berlin they said, "Conducting starts where everything else leaves off." So, I got swollen lips from playing the French horn, and then you have to go like this to play the oboe, and then my left arm ached from playing the violin. Still, in this institute I played percussion and played it with a vengeance. Once we played the *William Tell Overture,* which has a lot of cymbals in it. I was quite nearsighted and didn't have any glasses in those days, so I was banging away. Now you should know that you get a complex when people think: "Women aren't strong enough" or something like that, so I banged away and this conductor whom I could barely see was waving like this. I thought, he can't stop me, I'll show him! So I got up all my strength and banged and banged and banged. Finally he stopped the whole orchestra and said, "You, do you have to play so loud?"

In New York I heard about Richard Wagner. This person said to me, "Wagner, do you like him?" I said, "Let me tell you, I'm mad about him." Why? Well, you know that people have a habit of criticizing Wagner because he borrowed money that he didn't return, and he borrowed it because he was beside himself to get his operas mounted. You know, if I had one page of *Tristan* inside of me I would have knocked anybody down, stolen, begged, borrowed, anything—to get *Tristan* mounted!

Well, today my interviewer asked me what I was conducting at the Bowl on the 12th of July, and I told him among other things Wagner and

Sibelius, and, I went on, "Are you coming?" "Well," he said, "I'll come even though you're conducting Wagner." Isn't that dreadful? That's prejudice. I tell my children, my students, that they must learn modern music. When people say, "What do you like to conduct the most?" I say, "What I'm conducting at the moment. Certainly I have favorites, but you know that, even though Schoenberg was a modern composer, he made his students study traditional harmonies. So it's very unfair, when you have the strength over your students that you have—it's a very big thing to do to a little child—to say, "This awful modern music, what they're doing today is dreadful." You have no right to say that. You have to make them open-minded. You have to make them aware of everything. It's very interesting, Sibelius was one of my great masters. Now Sibelius didn't care much for Wagner. It wasn't that he hated Wagner, no, he didn't hate him, it was more like water running off a duck's back. Wagner just didn't say anything to him. Well, people told Sibelius that he had to go to Bayreuth, that he had to hear "that man from Bayreuth," that's what they used to call him, sometimes in very disparaging tones, so Sibelius went to Bayreuth, and when he said that he didn't hate Wagner, it was really a worse slam than hating him. Now Sibelius was the most independent composer there was at that time. Everybody else was drawn to the man from Bayreuth like a magnet, whether they knew it or not. Debussy was influenced by him, Richard Strauss was influenced by him, Bruckner was influenced by him, I can't begin to list all the people who were influenced by the man in Bayreuth. But Sibelius wasn't. He went his own way and his music has nothing, but nothing, of Wagner in it—no influence at all—that's the way it has to be when people are going to go an independent path. Yet I adore both these musicians madly.

I can't go into detail about how I got to go to Europe—that's a chapter all by itself. But I went and I worked and went as far as I could until the money ran out. Then I would take a job and go a little farther. All of this was to get nearer to New York. The only way you could do that was to go to Europe—Germany—to study. Finally I managed to see Dr. Karl Muck. By then I had these three letters of introduction to him, very important letters. Dr. Karl Muck was then the Director General of the Wagner Festival in Bayreuth and an internationally known Beethoven-Wagner conductor. So I had these three letters of introduction; in Europe such letters are very very important. So I went to Bayreuth and I presented the three letters. He looked at me, "From California? A girl? You want to be a conductor?" Nice, huh? Nice beginning. I said, "Yes, and yes, and yes." He said, "Well, the least I can do is to give you tickets to all the music dramas." Oh, was that a plus? They cost thirty marks then, ten dollars each, an absolutely enormous amount of money in 1927. So I got all of these, and yet I was not satisfied, never satisfied. He conducted *Parsifal,* and other conductors conducted *The Ring,* and so on.

In Bayreuth you can't see the conductor when he is conducting. Nor can you see the orchestra; it's a hidden orchestra. Instead of the orchestra going up, it goes way under the stage, so way back and under there is where the brass was and the six harps and eight horns and all of that enormous sound. The advantage of that was that the music sounded absolutely gorgeous; the trombones could blast their heads off and it did not affect the singing at all. You could still hear it. It was both deafening and beautiful. The conductors, of course, didn't make all these fancy gestures because nobody saw them. I hate to say it but some of my colleagues really do jump around on the podium. When I conduct like this, you see, people say aren't you afraid of falling? I say, "No, because we were taught in Berlin to plant our feet on the floor and don't move." Some of my colleagues go like this, and they go like that, and some of them even jump rope up and down. You've seen it. You know. Anyway, in Bayreuth you couldn't see the conductors. So I said to Karl Muck, "Oh please, I want to see you so badly, I want to see you conduct so badly. How can I do it?" He said, "Well I'll put you in the pit. You come to a rehearsal once, and you go down into the pit. So he put me in the pit, way down below with these six horns and eight harps. Now I was very impressionable, and he was doing *Parsifal*. Well if you haven't heard *Parsifal*, I know this sounds terrible, prejudicial to you, but I swore I would never hear *Parsifal* again in my life because I had heard it twenty-five times with the greatest conductor in the world, and I didn't want to disturb that memory. The effect was something tremendous. Imagine being there and hearing the end of the transformation scene—the end of *Parsifal*—oh me, oh my, it was so tremendous! I was shaken, absolutely shaken to the core of my being. And let me just throw this out: You *have to be* shaken; you have to want something *desperately;* when pupils of mine say, "Well I don't really know if I want to be a musician," I say, "Don't. If you don't know, and if you don't have the desire, the mad, passionate desire to let nothing and nobody come between you and your desire, then don't."

THE MIRACLE OF A GREAT MAN AND GREAT MUSIC

All right, so now I was so shaken by that music that I went straight to his house. Now Dr. Karl Muck lived only two blocks away from the theatre (on Parsifal Street). I went there, and he had a house frau to take care of him, and I rang the bell, just as I had every single day until he started to give me lessons. Bless his heart! I'd pestered him so long that out of sheer self-defense he gave me the lessons. There was absolutely nothing else he could do to get rid of me. Well, I went there, went in, and threw myself on the bed and sobbed and sobbed and sobbed. The house frau said, "But Frau Brico, what are you crying about? Maybe he just couldn't get you in tonight." I cried and cried. "Well, maybe he'll let you in tomorrow or the next day but it isn't always possible for him to do everything." I cried and cried and cried. She went on and on about why he might not have let me in. Finally I said, "But I was there." "What are you crying about?" She simply could not understand the depth of emotion that comes from the miracle of having heard a great man and great music.

After the summer was over, Dr. Muck said you must go to the Berlin Academy's conducting school. There were entrance examinations for the Academy and there were twenty applicants. Two got in and by some miracle I was one of them. There was one boy and one girl. The whole conducting school was only seven students, five in one class and we two in the other. So I said to myself, "Well, if you weren't meant to be a conductor you wouldn't have gotten into this school." Do you see what I'm driving at now? If this is worth anything at all, then just tell yourself, and tell your students—have blinders like horses, have blinders—don't look to the right or to the left, set your goal and follow it. Whether there was heartbreak in my life (and there was plenty of it) or not, it did not matter to me.

My friend the interviewer said to me, "If you had it to do over would you still like to be a conductor?" I said "Yes" because, as I have said to thousands of people, "I would rather die trying than not try at all." So there I was in Berlin and I had taken the next step. Wasn't that marvelous?

Well this went on and on and I graduated from Berlin and was able to conduct the Berlin Philharmonic. Then my dear darling beloved University of California brought me back for some concerts in San Francisco and in Berkeley. Then the Hollywood Bowl sneaked in and said we want her for an American premiere, and the University said, "No, *we* brought her back." They said, "Either you let her come here for the premiere or she doesn't get to conduct at all." Of course, I said, "Oh please, please, please, don't get mad just because I wasn't in San Francisco first." So I conducted here. Now you can see how each of these individual steps went on and on and on. And as I said, it has worked out despite the heartbreaks, despite everything, despite the difficulty, because it turned out that it wasn't just whether or not you knew what you were doing. No, prejudice has done many tragic things in the world. You may say, "Oh, that's just a musician talking, a crazy musician, but I say that if Hitler, Mussolini, Stalin, and Churchill had played string quartets together there never would have been a World War II."

I haven't even talked about one of the greatest influences on my life: Albert Schweitzer, the great humanitarian who was four times doctor and an enormously gifted organist. I haven't said a word about him, and the fact that I studied with him over a period of fifteen years both in Africa and in Alsace Lorraine. I met him first in Aspen, where some enterprising person wanted to make a big ski resort. As you know they certainly succeeded. Well, this person wished to celebrate an anniversary, a 200-year anniversary of Goethe's birth, and they celebrated by asking the greatest scholars in the world to come to Aspen, including Schweitzer who came from the middle of Africa. They asked him to come and to give two lectures. Of course this was right on my doorstep, and I was beside myself with joy. I tried to get everybody I knew to go, but he hadn't been made famous yet by *Time-Life*. You and I both know how publicity works, so I only got a couple of my students to go. Well, to meet him once was to want to see him all the time. So sometime I'll come back here, and I'll tell you a whole lot more about Albert Schweitzer, but now I think that I have to open up the subject of this little talk, this funny little talk, and to see if you have any questions, anything you're interested in.

Q. What would you say to a woman, let's say an oboe player or a flute player, who never becomes first chair; it seems like they're always second, third or fourth. What does that mean to you?

A. Any person, I don't care if he's yellow, black, woman, or man who wants to get somewhere, if they are proficient and if they try, then they will get somewhere. Now they are now doing what I suggested years ago when I founded the New York Women's Symphony Orchestra. I suggested that we have auditions behind screens so that you couldn't see who was playing, and that is just what is happening now. And there are women who become first chair. There is an oboe player named Lois Wann who was my oboe player in the New York Women's Symphony. She is playing even today. There are women first chairs. I want to say right now that I am not "women for the sake of women," not a feminist to the extent of "rah, rah women," no, *nein, nicht*. But I think it's terrible if anyone is black, yellow or what, who says, "Give me a chance, I need this chance."—Only if you deserve it—then you should have it. You know we were nice enough in the New York Women's Symphony to allow some men in. Why not? Why not? All I wanted to do by forming that women's symphony was to prove that women could play in every category of the orchestra. When I proved that, then I changed it to a mixed orchestra because men and women mix in life and they should mix in orchestras too. That is my philosophy; I don't care who applies, whether it's a man or a woman or a she or a he or what, if that person is good enough (and they should audition behind screens) then they should be chosen. Music is not relegated to one sex or another. You're either gifted or you're not gifted, and if you're gifted then you shouldn't be having things put in your way. I think it's tragic, absolutely tragic, when people say to me, "Oh, but a woman can't play a trombone," or "Oh, a woman can't play a French horn." Look, who knows the name of Kirsten Flagstad? Or another singer, what's her name, Birgit Nilsson. Do you really think that it takes more strength to sit comfortably in a chair with the music in front of you and blow a trombone or a French horn than it does to cavort around a stage singing by heart a role like Brunhilda or Aïda? Do you *really* think that takes more strength? When they talk to me about women not having strength I tell them I have the greatest timpani player in the world. She is worthy of playing with any major symphony, but she had to go to Wall Street and get a secretarial job. She was a marvelous timpanist with loads of strength and got special criticisms from the *New York Times*. She was absolutely magnificent, yet she couldn't get a job. I think nowadays she probably would.

Q. As a conductor how much control do you have over programming, and what have you done as far as playing compositions that happen to be written by women?

A. I have conducted women's compositions. You have a woman composer here in Los Angeles, a very fine composer. Her name is Elinor Remick Warren. She has had her things played widely, and I have played some of her work. Then there is another woman composer in New York, Joyce Barthelson, and I am going to conduct one of her works in Washington, D.C. I am certainly going to conduct women's compositions, but you must realize that when today's women composers should have been studying there wasn't any opportunity for them and they weren't always as tough and stubborn and Dutch as I am. And when they were supposed to be attending babies and this and that many of them felt, "What's the use of trying to study composition when I'll never get a chance to get my things heard?" There wasn't much encouragement, see? Of course women composers are perfectly capable, but what was the use of doing it if there was no chance to get your things performed? That's the way they felt.

Q. Besides conducting and studying, did you compose anything yourself?

A. Well, I had to do composition in order to get through my theory classes at the University of California and I did compose a movement of a symphony and some other things. But I felt there was enough good music written that I didn't need to add my bit. No, I am definitely a creative person in the way of creating music that has already been written, but not involved in writing it.

Q. Did you always have confidence in your talent?

A. What??!!! Did I have what???

Q. Did you always know you had the talent?

A. I don't know anything about talent. I just wanted to conduct. I said that from the beginning. I wanted to conduct and I believed that I could if I had the training. I didn't have father, mother, sister, brother, husband, children, but I did have the greatest training in the world and the greatest teachers in the world. I'll close with this statement. If you want to do something you can't just say, "I want to do it." You have to be prepared. You have to study. As a woman you even have to know five times as much as a man. You have to believe in what you're doing. You don't say, "Do I have talent?" You say, "I want to do it. I'm going to leave no stone unturned to better myself. I want to do it, and I will do it." Let that be my final word to you. "Prepare, and then do it." Thank you ladies and gentlemen.

MIND, MATTER AND MENTORS

THE MAKING OF A SOCIOLOGIST

CYNTHIA FUCHS EPSTEIN

Queens College, City University of New York

INTELLECTUAL DEVELOPMENT AND TRAINING

THE ASSIGNMENT FOR this series was an ambitious one: the location of sociology today, my place within it, and my intellectual development. Needless to say I will condense, and focus on some parts—those which I think are important.

My dreams as a girl never included a fantasy of traveling to other countries and seeing my books on the shelves of scholars there and discussing my research with them, a recent experience of mine. In fact I never imagined myself a writer of books at all. I had kept away from writing because my best friend was a short story writer and I shied from competition with her. So I kept my interests to the political and historical. Actually my fantasies ran mostly to achieving the heights of vicarious pleasures as a contemporary Madame de Stael. I imagined I could marry some articulate and poetic rich man and maintain a salon to which I would invite the brilliant minds of the era, providing good food and a good ear.

That was the dominant fantasy. Flights of fancy at various times revealed me as Wonder Woman or an abandoned princess who had been left at the doorstep of my unappreciative parents. In fact my mother caught on to this last fantasy and taunted me for many years by calling me Cinderella, mocking my dream of being discovered as the *true* princess. My fantasies were all passive fantasies, appropriate to the sex role designation of my generation: to be revealed, to be discovered, or to revel in the brilliance of others. I never imagined that by my own mind or hands I could achieve the exalted position to which I aspired. This was in spite of the fact that my father liberally bestowed on me books containing the biographies of great women, particularly great Jewish women: Deborah in the Bible, the poet Emma Lazarus whose poem is engraved on the Statue of Liberty, and the socialist Rosa Luxemburg. I suppose these had impact, however, because they exposed me to the idea that women could be doers and movers although I was terribly insecure about my own competence to move or do anything.

Many people today insist that role models provide a framework which creates identification; and that early conditioning sets aspirations and motivation. I had some of those. One was an outstanding teacher in the third grade, a woman by the name of Ruth Berken, who still designs curricula for New York City public schools. Berken gave us research projects to do in the third grade, visited our homes to know our environments, argued that we stand straight and not depend on the artificial constraints of girdles and bras. She was the first teacher I had in an experimental program for presumably "intellectually gifted" children (the IGC). This was a rather exciting but also quite intimidating program in which one was immersed in a sea of precocity of large ideas in small bodies. I suppose that what I came away with from this program was a set of intellectual standards and tastes, a real nose for the person who could generate and defend ideas best, as well as a good dose of humbleness. I, like many others in my classes (although I was sure it was only me), was made to realize that intellectual activity often didn't provide closure; and that there were a lot of smart people around who were always set to challenge. I ended up with a feeling of enormous insecurity with strains of megalomania—an impossible combination which made me view the future with some trepidation. Unlike the syndrome identified by Matina Horner, I had no fear of success but a fear of *failure,* and that fear often stood in the way of putting myself in competitive situations or even striving very hard. I don't think this syndrome is any more characteristic of women than it is of men, for I see it in certain of my male colleagues as well as my son, who decided not to play chess because the thought he might lose so terrifies him.

Perhaps Ruth Berken was a role model for me, as were my IGC classmates, many of whom have gone on to a certain fame in other fields and disciplines in the arts and sciences and world of letters. But they also seemed so impressive, I don't think I ever identified with them in any classic way. Rather, they made me scared to fall behind. My mother also played her part in this strange process which, in truth, or in the selective recall I offer as the answer to my assignment today—to report on my intellectual development—was not as a positive role model, but quite the opposite. My mother was a housewife who downgraded her own capacities, whose own fears prevented her from pursuing her talents, and because of her social and economic situation, she retreated into a world of domesticity and the local community. That is, she wasn't forced to confront her own fears and lived with feelings of inadequacy, a classic female pattern. But it also made her push for the idea that women should become competent, not necessarily in a real career, but in a steady occupation just in case things should go wrong. I somehow got the message from my mother that, as likely as not, things might very well go wrong, and therefore I came to believe it was important to have an occupation, to not depend on a husband, parents, or anyone else. So, in a sense it wasn't positive identification that pressed me, but negative role models and negative messages. It made me convinced in my later sociological thinking that perhaps motivation is created by a more complex web than we acknowledge, and that fears as well as rewards act to orient people to good things as well as bad things.

DOING GOOD AND DOING SERVICE

I might also note that my family was one in which there was a general orientation toward doing good and doing service. Both parents were active members of charitable and political organizations. My childhood world was sprinkled with causes and marches and fund-raising events. My household was an embodiment of the Protestant ethic.

I mention some of the various themes, strains, and contradictions in my early years because I am distressed at the somewhat linear view many psychologists have offered us in viewing the development of people. My experiences were not consistent; my choices were not necessarily rational; unanticipated consequences flowed from chance events.

Later experiences also certainly were as important to me as those early orientations and early fears. The choice of Antioch College turned out to be a good one, not only because I found a lot of intellectually kindred souls there, but because I became attached to a group of students in political science who were studying then with Professor Heinz Eulau. Eulau frightened a lot of people, but I was used to being frightened, and it didn't occur to me to buck authority. I was frightened, but I was also exulted by this brilliant man, who made each class an experiment; who assigned us weekly essays on our readings—which included a wide range of thinkers such as George Herbert Mead, Freud, Merton, Kecskemeti, Lasswell, Marx, and Darwin. Eulau had attracted a group of students who took pleasure in the constant intellectual interaction and interchange which his classes offered; who with him sought the use of theoretical exploration to find new explanations for what caused the different varieties and clusterings of human behavior. In fact, of that group of about ten or twelve, a good proportion today are professors in the social sciences with outstanding reputations. Several went on to become rather dynamic lawyers in the public interest law sector. Eulau was, as you see, one of those facilitators of excellence Robert Merton has written about.

It was also through Eulau that I was able to get a scholarship to the University of Chicago Law School—an abortive experience since I found law to be incompatible with my humanistic-behavioral orientation, and because my husband and I both had unrealistic views of how we could manage on a small amount of savings, and no income; because by then he, a former newspaperman, had decided to go back to graduate school. I might note that I chose law school through no great motivation, but because the scholarship was there, because I hadn't thought about graduate education in my field of political science, and because I didn't know what I wanted to do or could do. I, like many of my sisters today, thought of law as a field of learning which turned one into a real professional, that is to say, a lawyer, a person with a marketable profession.

I carried the burden of guilt heavily on my shoulders as I left after only six months. I wondered how I could hold my head up and felt that I had let all women down by my decision. I can't remember any more why my husband and I were so very discouraged—he in his field and I in mine. But I do know that there wasn't much in the way of channels of communication, of support or guidance available that *we knew about*. The experience certainly raised my consciousness regarding information, how tracking is accomplished, what it means to be an insider and an outsider, and how people themselves come to make the self-exclusionary moves to water down their dreams and make unfulfilling compromises.

Tails between our legs, my husband and I both came back to New York, our place of growing up, and took the kinds of jobs liberal arts college graduates take. He, who aspired to become a reporter for the *New York Times,* got a job for the house organ of the taxicab industry. I got a job as a secretary. In fact, that was the first of a series of jobs I held for organizations with social purpose. I spent three years with an organization which raised millions of dollars a year for hospitals and training programs. The women at the top were high-powered executive types. They came in early in the morning and left late at night; they vied for power and control of the organization; they had strong ambitions of a personal nature and also for the organization. Although they were counted by the U.S. Census as housewives, since they did not work for money, they were as involved and active as any IBM executive.

I suppose I had been asking questions about the place of women in society since childhood since my own searching led me to consider what being a woman meant in the society and, as a woman, what options there were for me to develop as a person. The experience in this women's organization showed me clearly that while there were ongoing myths about women's nature and ability to control, dominate, and seek fame and notice, women's performance simply did not match the myth.

SELF-SEARCHING

After three years of working in this organization and going to the New School at night for a degree in sociology, I decided to go to Columbia University for a Ph.D. This was after a lot of self-searching and guilt; I didn't want to give up the autonomy of making money, or to put a burden on my husband, who was also starting a new career. At this point my parents agreed to help me. They decided I was serious.

I chose Columbia because it was in New York and the best school in New York. I did not know it had one of the finest sociology departments in the country. It was by chance that one of my first courses was with William J. Goode, who excited my imagination by his cross-national, cross-historical approach to family sociology and the way in which his theoretical interpretation opened the puzzles of odd practices people exhibited in this context. The chance to work for him came a bit later, and I helped do the research for books on changes in family structure and on a propositional inventory of the family.

From Robert Merton I became entranced with the ways in which role theory and systematic analysis opened explanation into other perplexing arenas. I remember now thinking about the situation of women and making notes (notes which I later used in my book, *Woman's Place*) when he discussed the articulation of roles, the problems of cross-cutting status sets, and sex-role stereotyping. I suppose I carried pieces of the book I was later to write in my head for years, and I plugged the situation of women into whatever theoretical framework or methodology was offered as part of the Columbia curriculum. With each application I could see more.

I went to Columbia in 1960. I remained a student for a long time because I took on various teaching and research jobs in between, and because I was afraid of taking my comprehensive exams. In between I had a baby. In 1966 I was working on a dissertation about women lawyers because I became interested in what happened to women in a male-dominated profession, when Betty Friedan started the National Organization for Women (NOW). Added to my other role obligations as teacher and student, as mother and research assistant, I also became an activist. I rode the bus to Albany with Friedan, with Kate Millet, with Ti-Grace Atkinson and with Flo Kennedy to picket the legislature, and I wrote testimony to support new guidelines for the EEOC interpretation of the antidiscrimination laws.

I was not an activist for long. It became clear to me soon that my larger contribution would be on the scholarly side. But it has been through interchanges between the scholarly and activist worlds, as well as keeping an eye on what has been happening to woman's position, that I think my work has developed. The sociological ideas which seemed so perfect earlier for looking at role conflict, role assignments, and the problems of definition, were now growing into other areas of a broader character. I became increasingly aware that the second-ranking place of women was not just an accident of fate and the fact that women had to have babies and thus were not available for other jobs, or that combining the jobs was too difficult, but that there seemed to be a systematic patterning to the ways in which women were suppressed. The mechanisms of domination which abounded in male-dominated occupations also worked in female-population occupations. They were also going on in the family and in cultural life. Even in the microinteractions of everyday encounters that Goffman and his colleagues write about and which constitute one of the new and exciting subspecialties of sociology today, women faced controls which placed them and kept them in subordinate positions. Whether it was the insistence of the culture that they be shorter, stupider, and poorer than the men they chose to speak with or live with, or the argument that they were nobler, more tender, or more emotional than the men in their lives and therefore ought to segregate themselves from much of their daytime life, women were made agents in their own exclusion and their own domination. Women wanted the men in their work life or love life to be better than they. They wanted, and they were instructed, to "look up to a man."

Let me stress here that I am not talking only about early socialization experience, but the ongoing social process. Even in encounters with strangers, women learned an etiquette of submissiveness and were subject to microcontrols of the lifted eyebrow, the putdown.

Why, I asked, was this true? I have decided that because women constitute the largest threat to male domination, intertwined as they are with the lives of men, gatekeepers of society invests much in keeping them down. In fact, as I learned through observing and studying the lives of women in professional life, the reinforcing or punishing experiences in adult life often act to substantially change the self image and aspirations of women.

In current work I have spent some time analyzing theoretical frameworks and how they affect cultural views of women's place, as well as the ways in which they affect social science research and observation. It seems to me that we have not been sufficiently aware of the ways in which social science itself is affected by stereotyping. I began to think about this when I directed my focus to an analysis of women and success for a conference on women in science which was held at the New York Academy of Sciences. Of course Matina Horner's work had been getting quite a lot of attention at that time and there was much conceptual explanation in the air regarding the notion Horner identified as women's "fear of success." Horner's work suggested that the fears women have go back to their early socialization. It fit in generally with the focus on early socialization and its importance, and with our increasing awareness of sexist terminology in text books and in the media.

THE NEGATIVE EFFECT OF EARLY
SOCIALIZATION THEORY

But I fear that we have put too much weight on this way of thinking. As I suggested before, I think focussing too much on early socialization has negative consequences. Once we believe all the damage is done early, we can then write off an entire generation as incapable of being changed. It permits gatekeepers in the academy, business, and the professions to pass the buck to the primary school teachers who made girls take cooking while the boys took science. "Not our fault," they assert, "that women aren't trained to become administrators and heads of departments. They were socialized to be passive, docile, and retiring."

Now, no doubt some of this is true. But I have devoted myself in recent times to challenging the early socialization model—hardly original with me but underrepresented, I believe, in current thought, both popular and scientific. The alternative is a model of ongoing development—the framework which asserts that personality is not set early and is therefore unchangeable but that it is capable of change through a person's lifetime, and quite radical change at that.

I believe that the reason why it appears that personality is set early is because people are tracked in channels where they are not apt to receive different messages later in life than they had early; that, once having been labeled as being of a particular personality type and having a particular capacity, structure conspires to reinforce that view.

My initial cues regarding this model came when, after the women's movement had been sufficiently developed to make career opportunities available to many women, I could see distinct changes in the personalities of women. Those who had severe self-doubts regarding their own competence found that, when they were given additional responsibility, they could handle it well, although they were frightened to begin with. Women who were afraid of taking on new jobs normally reserved for men found they could not only learn things they thought they couldn't (like the economics of magazine production), but they found they liked the new activity. They also liked the power and they liked the success. Nothing, it seems, succeeds like success.

Of course, women with no science training cannot become nuclear physicists overnight. But there are many, many jobs, particularly managerial and administrative, for which most learning occurs on the job, and the only requisite is sufficient intelligence and motivation. What is needed is a lot of support and confidence on the part of those who assign the job, and reinforcement from others in the environment.

I have been gathering both historical and social psychological experimental data to corroborate this thinking, and have begun to reanalyze the work of Erikson, Piaget, and others who have been responsible for the emphasis on early socialization and developmental stage theory. Jerome

Kagan of Harvard is one of those who has contributed interesting work to show that significant advances in learning can occur far later than we have believed possible. Of particular significance is his work observing Guatemalan Indian children who are reared with little stimulation in the early years of life and are listless, passive, and uncommunicative. He asserts that children of eleven in the same environment who suffered the same paucity of stimulation, when challenged in peer group settings later in childhood, become animated and assertive, some even assuming dominance. It is the later stimulation and opportunity which creates this change, Kagan asserts. I think the lesson is instructive for those considering the question of women's abilities to use opportunities available through Affirmative Action programs.

This attention to early socialization has been just one of the areas I have considered in looking at the consequences of theoretical orientations and research work in the social sciences for the analysis of not only women, but for society as well. Last summer I was asked to write a paper which would contemplate the field of sociology, had women not been virtually excluded from it. Originally I had not thought there would be much difference. But let me share with you some of the other issues which arose in that analysis.* I was led to believe, after some thinking, that the social sciences have given us an incomplete and probably distorted view of reality because of the systematic inattention to the place and participation of women in social life. I devoted attention to both the modes of analysis and the particular sub-fields whose character has been most affected by the exclusion of women.

Of course, any view of reality is to some degree subject to the perspective of a particular group. The goal, always, is to strive for objectivity by cutting through one's cultural or chauvinistic blinders. What has passed for scientific objectivity in sociology has often fallen short of that standard. The failure of objectivity which results from what may be called the male perspective is only one of many, but it is an important one.

Most descriptions of society have been recorded and analyzed by men and have centered on the world of male endeavors.

Some sociologists argue that, even if true, the social sciences' focus on men has not given an inaccurate profile of society. After all, men dominate and shape the structures of society; therefore, the study of major institutions is properly the study of male decisions, and men are the proper subjects of such studies.

In some spheres this is probably correct. The more convincing argument is that, although much work in sociology is done by men, it is not gender-specific, and the findings have contributed to our understanding of *all* groups.

---

*For a more complete analysis see my "A Different Angle of Vision: Notes on the Selective Eye of Sociology," in *Social Science Quarterly* (December, 1974), 645-656.

The latter view was held by most sociologists, women and men, until fairly recently, when it was challenged by the work of feminist scholars and others in the women's movement.

THE CONSEQUENCE OF MALE BIAS

Although I, too, have become increasingly more sensitive to the lurking presence of male bias in sociology, I do not believe there are essentially different male and female perspectives. Rather, it is clear to me that to the extent that the profession's work *has* been *male*-oriented, it has been skewed and is therefore wrong; the same would have resulted from work done from a "female" perspective.

That sociology had no right to its claims of scientific objectivity had been heard from other quarters long before the criticism in the women's movement, but the feminist critique identified the bias of gender, whereas the others were more concerned with what they believed to be political bias.

Alice Rossi suggests that the omission of women from social science investigation stemmed from general analytical problems and the structure of the social sciences themselves. Commenting on Simone de Beauvoir's analysis of the place of women in society in her book, *The Second Sex*, and on the lack of serious attention it received when it first appeared in the 1950's, Rossi suggests that de Beauvoir's eclectic interdisciplinary approach was at odds with the narrow specialization characteristic of the social sciences at that time.

It was not that one could only study women if one were a generalist, but that women were ignored by the specialists, none of whom specialized in *them*.

I would go on to argue that sociological *methods* have not been specifically deficient with regard to women, but they are *generally* deficient in that they have not alerted us to what have been the gaps in our knowledge about any group, whether women, minorities, the elderly, or children.

I believe that the methodological and theoretical perspectives offered in ethnomethodology, structural-functional analysis (with its focus on systemic analysis), conflict analysis, and other approaches used by sociologists pose no intrinsic limitations for the analysis of women in society. Rather, the problem has been that most social scientists of these conceptual persuasions have not considered women to be important or interesting topics of study. The few who have do not complain of special theoretical or methodological difficulties.

The "methods" are variable, of course, in their specification and their precision. None give a formula for an all-embracing description and analysis of social groups or social processes, and boundaries of groups or institutions must be arbitrarily drawn. The fact is that there is no real agreement, for example, on how classes are constituted, or even on what power or influence is. This lack of agreement affects the analysis of women as it affects the entire field of sociology.

As Rossi suggested, analysis may (1) be so specialized that the whole is lost, or (2) so selective that certain parts never come to the sociologist's view. This is partly a question of values and of fashions in values. The central value here is that women have been undervalued and that little attention has been directed to their existence in the sciences, in politics, in art, or in literature. Recalling the not-too-distant past, not only was it unfashionable for sociologists to study women, but women sociologists were often warned against choosing research topics dealing with women because this path would not lead to professional success. Indeed, there is some evidence that it was hard to get such research funded and also that it was hard to interest professors in the supervision of such dissertations.

The value problem was further exacerbated by the fact that *younger* researchers who were not bound to "establishment" norms were also not convinced that women were a group worthy of attention. The more radical of them (who might have been more sensitive to the position of an underclass than were established sociologists) felt the more pressing problems were those of the poor and the blacks. Few, if any, of them saw women as an equally disadvantaged group.

This phenomenon has persisted, although in some quarters the debate over priorities does continue. Ironically, politically radical sociologists have exhibited considerable backsliding on the question since the time of Engels, who wrote more sensitively and perceptively about the position of women than do many radical men today. Many radical sociologists have assumed methodological and conceptual blinders on the matter because, incorrectly, they identify the women's movement as a middle-class movement unworthy of their attention. Thus, the radicals' bias, in favoring the most modish underdog, has been found in curious alliance with the bias of the profession's establishment. One must remember, too, that these stylistic prejudices are not limited to male sociologists but have been held as well by female researchers.

THEORETICAL MODELS AND THEIR CONSEQUENCES

Like much of our day to day thinking theoretical models are also the products of fads and fashions. Certain models have had major consequences for the analysis of women as well as of society as a whole; as I outlined above, the early socialization model is one of them. There is the assumption that the personality is formed early in life and is thereafter relatively unmalleable; this has created blinders to the impact of socialization after early childhood and of social control systems throughout the life cycle. It is a static rather than a processional model. I will not direct more attention to that model since I discussed it earlier, but let me indicate another way in which models distort perceptions. A good model should alert the researcher to seeing things he or she might not have thought of before. A poor model tends to limit the range of data, or to orient the researcher to see things only in a way which is consistent with the model.

Let me give you an everyday example of what I see as the way girls' and boys' behavior is viewed, that is, seen physically, by social scientists. The models of masculinity and femininity in American culture hold that boys are aggressive and girls are passive; that boys bear hardships with a grimace and control their emotions, while girls give vent to emotions by crying.

My own findings as a participant observer in this society, in organizations entirely run by women, and as a somewhat systematic observer of children's play groups, indicate that girls or women can be, and are, as aggressive, or more aggressive, than boys or men, and that boys are also apt to cry at being physically hurt or at having their feelings hurt. Furthermore, in a decade and a half of professional academic activity I have never seen a woman colleague cry in public. After all, crying, except at funerals, is unusual for adults in American culture, whether women or men. Yet, even feminists share the culture's assumptions when they *defend* women's rights to be emotional and ask that men be allowed to be so too. They also sometimes insist that women are kinder, more caring, and more nurturant. The defense too often rests on the same biased assumption as the attack: that women are emotional whereas men are not, and that the capacity to work, or love, is sex-linked.

Sociologists tend to work with a theoretical or cultural assumption and to then search for corroborating data. I know of few studies in which the play of boys and girls, in natural settings, has been carefully observed and quantified. Sociologists often have not been aware of "what is going on" either because they can't see what they have decided is not there, or because their perceptual framework demands that they label their observations to fit their theory.

SELECTIVE VISION IN SUBSTANTIVE FIELDS

Prejudice

Let me turn now to the exclusion of women from the sociological consciousness in some substantive areas of sociology and note some deficiencies of analysis which have followed. Considerable work has been done in sociology and social psychology on the nature of prejudice and discrimination, and some general hypotheses have emerged in which prejudice is considered as a phenomenon directed toward *minorities*. What more would we know about prejudice if we explored its existence against women—who are a majority of the population although they are kept at minority levels in certain spheres and institutional realms!

Certain propositions prevail in the sociology of minority-group relations indicating that the more contacts between the dominant group and minority group and the more they meet in shared tasks, the less the prejudice. However, the reverse has been observed about prejudice towards women. Though whites would rather work with blacks than play with them and have them as colleagues rather than members of their families, it is quite the reverse for women. Men would rather live and eat and sleep with women than work with them. The dominant white male class regards both women and blacks as inferior and less worthy to associate with in certain spheres. They are certainly viewed as inappropriate to hold superior positions.

Perhaps some social psychological research might have more bearing on the nature of prejudice if carried out under a more general theory of stratification. Some recent research indicates that oppressors tend to believe that their victims "deserve" what they get because they are inferior or deficient in some way.

In political sociology, although there has been research work on how women vote and why they vote as they do, there have been no studies which explore women's systematic exclusion from leadership positions. Some students of political sociology have "found" there are routes to power which only certain men are permitted to travel; they have not looked at the ways in which women were used in political campaigns, as legislative aides, and in a wide range of ancillary roles, often coming close to power yet remaining cut off from it. Although we know that mothers and mistresses of kings often wielded considerable behind-the-scenes power in other countries, it would be interesting to know whether American women have acted "politically" in this way. Of course, it is difficult to do research on any behavior which is secret or is undocumented. Women's general invisibility, whether in politics or in the professions, has meant that their contributions have typically been unseen. But few researchers have probed beneath this surface.

It is also clear that the political nature of women's subordination has not been studied by major political analysts or students of the dynamics of power. It is certainly "politics" when certain groups are kept down for the benefit of those dominant in the system.

Similarly, the sociology of stratification has neglected the position of women in the stratification system. Only recently, Joan Acker pointed out that "sex has rarely been analyzed as a factor in stratification processes and structures, although it is probably one of the most obvious bases of economic, political, and social inequalities." She and others have pointed out that social mobility patterns and trends on a societal level are based primarily on studies of white males, and she cites one of the most important of these works, Blau and Duncan's *The American Occupational Structure*. Their conclusions regarding stratification patterns in the United States cannot be correct because their analysis excludes women's role in the work force as well as the occupations in which women predominate. It is curious that studying male workers only seemed to these otherwise rigorous sociologists to be methodologically sound.

There are even greater gaps. I am convinced that the subjugation of women is a crucial element in the maintenance of power by elites because women constitute the largest pool of eligibles who could compete for elite decision-making places. In other work I have viewed the limits on women's occupational and political mobility as a "holding operation" of ruling elites and have attempted to consider how these mechanisms work against all groups who are potential competitors. I consider this perspective crucial to further analysis if we are to learn more about "who governs."

THE STRUCTURE OF THE PROFESSION AND
THE DIFFUSION OF KNOWLEDGE

The little work we have on the position of women in the social structure has been done predominantly by women sociologists. I have a suspicion that what women sociologists write is read more seriously by other women than by male sociologists. We can partly account for the phenomenon by considering, for a moment, the sociology of the profession of sociology. You, as I, can note the sex division of labor within the profession: women seem to cluster in certain fields (e.g., the family and sex roles), those which historically have not been viewed as the important or interesting ones. Furthermore, research reported on these fields has not, typically, appeared in the prestigious journals or been commonly cited.

Furthermore, the structure of social relations within sociology affects visibility. Even in recent times a good deal of intellectual exchange seems to be within sex lines, first, because women share a greater interest and a vested interest in research on topics relating to women, and second, because women sociologists feel that other women take their work more seriously than male sociologists do. Further, male colleagues typically hold more power than women colleagues, and rather than confront the inequity in informal social relations, women researchers feel more comfortable exchanging drafts of papers and reprints with each other.

But self-exclusion or insulation does not account for the fact that so many male sociologists are not aware of the research work of women sociologists. Men avoid those areas which they consider "women's studies" or that "women's lib stuff." Anyone attending sessions at professional meetings on sex role research or other topics presumably related to women can see that the audiences are populated with women. So are conferences which deal with research on the problems of women. The few men who attend are those whose own specialties are in the family or on male sex roles.

Other consequences flow from the fact that, although as students women have as much contact as the men with male professors, their chances of maintaining working relationships as colleagues are relatively much lower except in exceptional circumstances or because of affectional or sexual ties. The women sociologists writing today have been trained primarily by male mentors. However, in a field generally suffering from generational discontinuity, it is my impression that proportionately fewer women than men can be said to be disciples of the major figures in the field. The intellectual effects are clear; disciples typically test and refine the ideas of their mentors. They feed back and suggest new lines of development and new applications. Women have not been seen as colleagues, then, because they are not in the same structural positions as men, their ideas are not considered interesting and important, and they are often not heard and cannot be heard.

Furthermore, I suspect that not many male sociologists read the work of their women ex-students, particularly when the work is on women, although this has not been my experience with my own mentors, particularly Eulau, Merton or Goode. One indicator of this may be found in footnoting patterns. Women's works are probably footnoted proportionately less than the work of men, except by other women.

There are, of course, exceptions to these and there has been some change with the heightened consciousness of male sociologists in the field. My comments are based on my observations (although not always my experiences) and those of women colleagues. If they hold up, however, the implications are broad, suggesting not only a poverty of insight into the workings of society because of the poor documentation of women's roles and their interactions with men, but a poverty of real opportunity for a growing number of trained and competent women in the profession.

Research activity by women sociologists on women is relatively new. Because few women sociologists were actively working and recognized, most of the research on women was done under the rubric of Family Research, with contributions by a number of male sociologists as well as a few women. Among them were Robert Bell, William Goode, Marvin Sussman, Constantina Safilios-Rothschild, Mirra Komarovsky, and even the often criticized Talcott Parsons.

Some of these confined their work to family research. Others went on to analyze other social institutions and developed larger theories of society, but it seems curious that they often failed to carry their insights on the role of women into their more global work. Although both Parsons and Goode did so when they were talking about women within the context of the family, both failed to consider women as independent factors in their other analyses. Even Friedrich Engels, who wrote brilliantly on women's roles in the family, forgot to consider their specific roles as workers in his subsequent analyses of the labor force.

The failure of sociology to deal meaningfully with the place of women throws a harsh light on the insufficiencies of theoretical models that have shaped the profession's work for the past quarter-century. It is time new models were proposed or the old ones altered to provide an image of society less distant from reality. Events have made our sensitivities more acute and have enabled us to better understand the limitations of our theories and methods. Theoretical and methodological work on a more culture-free basis would provide us with new insights not only on the sociology of "woman's place" in society but on the sociological profile of the entire society and, indeed, of all social systems.

That is where I think the social sciences stand now, and where I think the most exciting work will be done. That is a rash statement, but it expresses a firm belief. A social science that excludes half the people of the earth is not better than a physical science that excludes the sky from the analysis of the earth or the earth from the analysis of the sky.

INVESTIGATING THE SOLID STATE

MILDRED S. DRESSELHAUS

Massachusetts Institute of Technology

Outline

PERSONAL INTELLECTUAL DEVELOPMENT

HISTORICALLY, THE FIELD of solid state physics and engineering has attracted few professional women (3 percent in physics, 1 percent in engineering). This underrepresentation of women has an important impact on the individual careers of women in these fields, and my case is no exception.

I was born to immigrant parents who had little formal education. My schooling through the ninth grade was in "underprivileged," biracial schools in New York City during the periods of the Great Depression and World War II. Though my education here was minimal in academic areas, I learned other things which later proved to be especially important: physical and emotional survival in hostile environments, independence, motivation and determination, self-discipline, a high aspiration level. In this period, my major objective was to rise above the restrictions and limitations of a ghetto environment, and these obstacles were much greater than any that I later faced in my professional career.

As a child, I knew few professionals of either sex, but the professionals I did encounter were mainly women—schoolteachers and our family doctor. It is perhaps worthy of comment that our family doctor was a Jewish woman war refugee, who practiced in our biracial community because this was the best opportunity she could find. In our community, it was the common practice for men, women, and children to work, in whatever capacity they could, to earn enough money for survival.

As I look back, it is clear that the critical point in my career occurred at age thirteen when I passed the entrance examination to Hunter College High School. It is likely that I was the first and only student from my ghetto school to gain entry into this select secondary school. On entrance, my formal educational level was significantly below that of my classmates, and I was deficient in the social graces as well. But my high motivation level more than compensated for these shortcomings. Since Hunter was an all-girl school, I never became aware that women were restricted in their career choices. In my case, college plans were determined by financial considerations, rather than educational opportunities or career objectives.

It was on this basis that I entered Hunter College to become an elementary schoool teacher, because this was clearly a field where there was ample employment opportunity. A turning point in my college career came in my second year through the intervention of a woman physicist who taught my atomic physics course and encouraged me to consider a career as a professional physicist. My undergraduate technical education was mediocre at best, but I did receive a great deal of personal encouragement and attention. The emphasis of the Hunter College staff on personal achievement and on service to society were probably more important in the end than were the technical deficiencies in my education. At that time the student body at Hunter College was mostly female, together with a few World War II veterans, who tended on the average to fall below the women students academically. This overall situation contributed to Hunter's supportive environment for the training of women professionals.

As a college senior, I was uncertain about whether to do graduate work in physics or in mathematics. My most attractive offer was for graduate study in mathematics, and I would probably have become a mathematician were it not for the Fulbright exchange program which came into existence at that time. An announcement of the Fulbright program on a bulletin board attracted my attention, and I proceeded to apply for a fellowship to study physics at the University of Cambridge, England. A year abroad had great appeal to me, because I had scarcely ventured beyond the confines of New York City up until that time. Thus, when a Fulbright fellowship was awarded to me, I felt unable to turn down the offer. So began my career in physics.

At Cambridge University I strengthened my undergraduate physics background. By this time I was far more uncertain about my academic ability than about my acceptance as a woman. I felt encouraged to find that I could hold my own in the competitive environment of Cambridge University, and later at Harvard (where I took my Master's degree) and at the University of Chicago (where I took my Ph.D. degree). It was at Chicago that I decided to become an experimental solid-state physicist, and this decision was made largely because research in this area could be carried out in a flexible way by the individual investigator. Many of my student colleagues considered this a surprising choice because the field of high-energy physics was at that time a far more popular and fashionable field, as well as an area of strength at the University of Chicago. In retrospect, my decision to enter solid-state physics was a wise choice, not only because of its more attractive lifestyle, but also because this was a newly emerging, exciting, and rapidly expanding field. Moreover, there were few qualified people to fill the many available positions.

My thesis work involved the study of the magnetic field dependence of the surface impedance of superconductors. The observation of some unusual and unexpected effects served to enhance my self-confidence and to give me some visibility in the research community. At this time there was an abundance of employment opportunities in this general research area, but my decision to accept a postdoctoral position at Cornell University was not made on the basis of scientific considerations, but rather because of my marriage to Gene Dresselhaus, who was a junior faculty member in the Physics Department at Cornell.

My two years at Cornell were not particularly productive scientifically. But this was largely irrelevant, because nepotism rules made it impossible for Cornell to employ both my husband and me. Therefore, we decided to join the staff at the MIT Lincoln Laboratory, which had excellent research facilities as well as an active research group and this laboratory would hire both of us. My seven years at Lincoln Laboratory were especially productive scientifically because of the excellent research environment in which I worked. It was during this period that our children were born, one during my last year at Cornell and the other three shortly after coming to Lincoln. Because our four children arrived within a five-year period, my working schedule was tied to the availability of babysitters. This created conflict because my schedule was often not consistent with the official laboratory hours. The irritation engendered by this situation eventually made me restless, and I was eager to accept a one-year visiting professorship in the Electrical Engineering Department at MIT when the opportunity arose. The appointment was made possible by a special fund provided by Abby Rockefeller Mauzé to bring women scholars to MIT. After one year, this visiting appointment led to a permanent appointment.

In this position I have had fine research opportunities, contact with excellent students in the classroom and in the supervision of their research projects, and opportunities for extensive administrative experience. My career in academia has been busy, exciting and stimulating, and far more interesting than I had ever imagined anything could be as a child. Whatever success I have achieved is largely due to encouragement and help from my husband, colleagues, family, babysitters, and children.

THE CREATIVE PROCESS IN SCIENCE AND ENGINEERING

Since my professional field includes both science and engineering, it seems appropriate to offer some comments on the discovery and creative process in both of these fields. A second reason for addressing both fields is connected with the professional directions of the other participants in this Frontiers of Knowledge series. My area of technical competence is in Solid-State Physics, which borders on the Physical Sciences on the one hand and the Engineering Sciences on the other. Research in these fields tends to be multidisciplinary in nature, and the trend for the future is in the direction of increasing interdisciplinary interaction. Since there are some differences in the discovery and creative process in science as opposed to engineering, I will discuss these two disciplines separately.

Research in science starts with the identification of a problem area. A suitable problem area offers promise for an interesting and rewarding scientific discovery and/or promise for technological applications. The identification of a problem area often involves inspiration, intuition, and imagination. Once the problem area is identified, a definition is made of the specific research problem to be solved. Here we set down the goals and objectives of the research and the basic approach that will be used in reaching these objectives. This aspect of the research process stresses a knowledge of previous research work in this area, if any, and a thorough knowledge of the broad fundamental principles that will play a role in the solution of the problem. The problem definition is often the most difficult part of the research project and has a flavor that is very different from the thought processes encountered in the classroom situation, where the problems to be solved are specified in the homework assignments.

Once the research problem has been defined, a plan of attack is adopted and the execution process is set into motion. This tends to be a long process where skill and hard work are necessary ingredients. This is a period of great frustration for research students, since the initial conception of a plan of attack seldom works out in all details. Almost every first-year research student goes through a period of frustration, often thinking that he or she is the only one having troubles, and the only one who is an incompetent. In this execution phase there is usually a reassessment of the problem definition and a reformulation of the plan of attack. Eventually the technical difficulties are solved and results begin to emerge. When the results finally do come, they seem to come thick and fast. It is not uncommon at this point to look back on the project and realize that if no blunders had been made, the problem could have been solved in perhaps one-tenth the time. On the other hand, to the professionals in science and engineering, the sensation of grappling with a difficult problem that one does not know how to solve provides a great deal of satisfaction beyond the frustration mentioned above. (A study of the dual feelings of frustration and satisfaction in scientists and engineers might provide a rewarding research topic for a psychologist!)

In my own research experience, I have found that most problems work out better than expected, and this kind of serendipitous success also provides a sense of satisfaction to the scientist.

One of the questions that often arises in scientific research is "When is a problem finished?" The end of a research project sometimes is well defined by the achievement of the original objective. But more often than not, the results of a research project suggest further work, which is often more extensive than the original problem definition. In this sense, the results of one research project can lead to the problem definition of a new research project. It is usually the more rewarding research projects that suggest further investigation. It does, however, take a certain amount of maturity and experience to decide whether further work will lead to new major discoveries or only to minor improvements.

Another component of the discovery process in both science and engineering is the communication of results to professional colleagues through publication in journals and oral presentations at professional society meetings. Many technical students are attracted to science and engineering because of the perceived emphasis on quantitative techniques and reasoning rather than on verbal skills. To be sure, mathematical and quantitative skills are essential to the execution of any research project in science and engineering. Nevertheless, verbal skills (both oral and written) form a very necessary ingredient for the communication of results and the dissemination of ideas.

Although the discovery process in science and engineering has a great deal in common, there are also many differences. The identification of a problem area in engineering is largely motivated by the identification of a societal need. As in science, the problem definition is crucial and often difficult. These difficulties are usually related to technical issues, though synergistic societal factors are becoming increasingly important. If a nuclear power plant is to be constructed, the engineer must be concerned not only with the technical issues involved in constructing such a plant, but also with societal factors governing the location of the plant, such as population distributions, safety issues, and ecological considerations. When a specific problem is defined in engineering, there are usually a number of possible solutions. That is, there are usually many ways to achieve a particular engineering goal, and the final choice for the plan of attack is made through an optimization procedure, with quality, cost and time being some of the more common parameters that must be considered. While the execution of science and engineering research programs has much in common, the time and cost aspects often are given relatively more attention in engineering research. Also, the completion of a research project tends to be more clearly defined in engineering than in science; when the engineering objective is achieved within the specified time scale, the project is considered finished. Still, in the execution of a particular engineering activity it is very often the case that either new technological needs are identified, which lead to the initiation of other engineering projects; advanced technological capabilities are developed which lead to further engineering and research and development opportunities; or new physical phenomena are encountered, which lead to further scientific research. Just as science provides the basic tools for the solution of engineering problems, engineering often stimulates basic scientific research that may become important as science or in the next generation of engineering applications.

THE SCIENTIST'S AND ENGINEER'S WINDOW ON THE WORLD

The scientist and the engineer look at the world through a window different from that of the humanist and the social scientist. In the humanities many of the great achievements made in the past are still very meaningful to us today. We still enjoy reading the classics, admiring ancient buildings, looking at Renaissance paintings, listening to baroque music. To many people, the achievements of today's humanists, though different, are not manifestly better, more profound, nor more beautiful than the contributions of past generations. The social scientist studies the past, is concerned about the present and thinks about the future. Still, the social science disciplines are tied to human beings, who do not change as rapidly from one generation to another as does their technology.

On the other hand, in science and engineering the emphasis is always on the future. We always want to do things better than we have done in the past. We are anxious to utilize more fully our available resources. Scientists and engineers have as their main objective a desire to improve the quality of life for present and future generations through technology. Nevertheless, these same scientists and engineers are often also responsible for the creation of new problem areas (pollution, depletion of natural resources, population explosion).

Science and engineering are constantly confronted with rapidly changing technologies, new ideas and concepts, new ways of doing things. Furthermore, the time scale for technological change has been steadily accelerating during the nineteenth and twentieth centuries. We can each recount the many important changes that have occurred in the course of our own lives or that of our parents: the automobile, the airplane, the radio, TV, the telephone, the computer, just to mention a few. Every scientist and engineer has faith that new inventions and discoveries are on the horizon and has a desire to play a role in the discovery process.

In recent years, both scientists and engineers have had to take a broader view of themselves and the world around them. First, scientific activity has moved towards larger-scale, multidisciplinary research projects which contrast with the entrepreneurial projects that dominated the scene in past decades. Second, today a significant fraction of the scientific research output comes from research groups where cooperative research is carried out by physicists, chemists, materials scientists, and engineers all working together, and often not cognizant of the boundaries between their nominal disciplines. Third, the scientist's view has also broadened because of the increasing interaction of science and technology with societal issues such as the energy crisis, the depletion of natural resources, and the development of systems for national defense. Finally, today's scientists are having to justify the value of their research contribution to the society that supports these research activities principally through governmental funding.

Current trends have also broadened the viewpoint of the engineer. In the engineering profession a broad, science-based background can provide many of the necessary tools for the solution of engineering problems. The recent experience of unemployment and obsolescence of engineers in the aerospace industry has underlined the need for a broad and thorough knowledge of the fundamentals of science and engineering principles and the dangers of overspecialization. Ironically, however, the tight job market also favors the specialist with previous experience closely matching a current job description. This, then, fosters the trend toward overspecialization. In principle, there is widespread support for continuing education and on-the-job training for engineers who need to be retooled; unfortunately, the resources to provide such opportunities are often not available.

Because of the increasing societal intervention in engineering management, either through regulation or legislation, today's engineers are becoming more aware of the social sciences and the problems of society. Because of the strong interaction between technology and business and the increasing competition in high technology industries, both at home and abroad, education in the principles of economics and management is becoming an essential field of study for today's engineering students.

LIFE-STYLE OF AN ENGINEER AND SCIENTIST IN ACADEMIA

Let us now take a look at the day-to-day activities of an engineer or scientist in academia. Of some significance is the observation that these professions are usually practiced in one of three sectors: the university, industry or government. For engineers, the industrial sector dominates, with government laboratories assuming a secondary role, and universities having the smallest representation. For scientists the university sector is relatively more important. When viewing the commitments of an engineer or scientist in academia, the availability of a large community of professional colleagues in a non-academic environment has an important effect on his life-style.

As for most academicians, engineering and science professors divide their time between teaching, research, administration, and other activities. The teaching obligations consist of giving lectures, directing recitation sections for smaller groups of students, as well as the informal teaching that takes place when students come to the professor for help with a specific problem or concept. In the science and engineering disciplines, professors tend to be available and on-campus for most of the workweek, and for this reason the informal teaching activities usually represent a major time commitment. Because of the nature of the subject matter, these informal interactions are of particular importance to the training of students.

The emphasis on research is perhaps greater in science and engineering than in other fields because of the rapidity with which technological change occurs. To be effective in classroom teaching, one must keep up with the field, and this implies activity in research. Individual participation in all aspects of research is the pattern of junior faculty members generally and senior faculty members at smaller universities. At the major research-oriented universities, the size of research groups tends to be larger and the senior professors assume more of a supervisory role. This means that the professors identify the problem areas, define the problems to be solved, and participate in developing the mode of attack, but seldom do more than supervise the actual execution of the research, which is carried out by graduate students as part of their research training. At the large research-oriented universities, the commitment to research is often greater than to the more formal teaching functions. On the other hand, research supervision is often indistinguishable from the informal teaching mode and is a very important part of the graduate education process.

The commitment of a faculty member to administration is probably independent of academic discipline. This work consists of committee assignments, attendance at various types of faculty meetings, counseling of students, and participating in the examination procedures for graduate students. A certain amount of administrative work also goes into running a research operation in terms of raising money for the research itself, providing support to graduate students, and writing reports for research sponsors.

A fourth category of activity for an engineering or science professor is termed "outside" activities, normally occupying one day per workweek, and these activities are of great importance to his or her own professional development. Under the heading of "outside" activities come consulting, professional activities, and government service. These activities offer opportunities for making contact with the latest technological developments, for developing collaborative research projects between university and industry, and for fostering personal contacts leading to future employment opportunities for students. The more senior and better-known faculty members often have extensive involvement in government service, render service to professional societies, or are on visiting committees to other universities and research laboratories, and participate in the refereeing of research manuscripts for professional journals. Various organizations, such as the National Science Foundation, the National Research Council, and the National Academies of Science and Engineering, depend upon strong inputs and time commitments from the scientific and engineering communities in order to carry out their missions.

WOMEN IN SCIENCE AND ENGINEERING

The nature of the science and engineering professions is such that the work to be done is not in any way sex-stereotyped, although there are few women professionals in either the physical sciences or engineering. Because my own research interest is in only the two fields of physics and engineering, I will restrict my comments to these fields, and emphasize that many of the following statements do not apply to women working in other disciplines. Because of the small numbers of women in engineering and physics, women are something of a curiosity and feel that they are individually very visible. On the other hand, men do not feel threatened by women physicists or engineers, and this may be one reason why women in these professions are exposed to relatively less job and salary discrimination than in other fields, though women do have less opportunity for promotions and advancement, particularly at the more senior levels. In science and engineering, women also benefit from the fact that it is possible to evaluate job performance objectively in these fields.

I frankly think that being a woman has often helped my career by making me more visible, and making my accomplishments more visible as well. It would, however, be fair to say that women in these fields suffer some job discrimination because men often do not take them seriously. Men often have doubts about the dedication of women to their work when it is in competition with the demands of husbands and children. This tends to be more of an emotional than a rational reaction to the situation. I am acquainted with at least one study which shows that Ph.D. women in physics who have family commitments tend to publish more papers than do male physicists; on this basis (and there is other supporting research) we may conclude that those few women who are dedicated enough to acquire a Ph.D. degree have a very serious commitment to their profession.

In the near future, we can anticipate a large increase in the number of women electing careers in science and engineering because of the better career and employment opportunities for women in these fields as opposed to other careers. A major increase in the number of women in the field would encourage men to take women scientists and engineers more seriously.

Women are now beginning to assume administrative positions in science and engineering. As a former woman engineering administrator (serving as Associate Department Head of the Electrical Engineering Department at M.I.T. for a two-year term), I am convinced that being a woman is no hindrance in carrying out the required administrative responsibilities. On the other hand, in talking with other women who have had similar kinds of administrative responsibilities, I perceive that we all feel under some special pressure to succeed so that other women will be considered for such leadership opportunities in the future.

THE FIELD OF SOLID-STATE PHYSICS AND ENGINEERING

Let us now consider from whence the field of solid-state physics and engineering came and where this field is going. The identification of this as a distinct research field can be said to be a post-World War II phenomenon, though much important work on the subject goes back many years before that. Because of the need for semiconductor diodes for microwave radar applications during World War II, great technological progress was made in the purification of semiconducting materials such as silicon and germanium. This great technological advance led to the discovery of the transistor in 1947. It is amazing to think that a tiny transistor which is about one ten-thousandth of a centimeter in size can give rise to the multi-billion dollar semiconductor electronics industry. The industrial interest in solid-state physics and engineering has contributed to the booming research era that this field has been experiencing from the early 1950's until the recent past.

To be sure, prior to World War II, important basic discoveries were made in this general field, such as the development of the free electron theory of metals and the discovery of superconductivity, just to mention a few. However, in the pre-World War II era, the focus of the research activity was largely university-based, and the pace of research was slow in comparison with today's rapidly changing technology. The great expansion of the solid-state field was brought about by the increased industrial interest and sponsorship of research programs, coupled with greatly increased governmental support for these research activities. The need for personnel to fill the many new research positions created by this expansion led to a major stimulation of university activity and research in these fields. As more people began to participate in research, the pace of research and development increased rapidly, and it is only lately that the rapid expansion of the recent past has stopped. Because of the sudden change in the growth pattern of science and engineering generally, many professionals have had to go through a difficult readjustment period that has adversely affected their morale. The decline in the number of new opportunities in science and engineering may serve to restrict the employment options for women, who tend to be latecomers to these professions.

Among achievements of the last two decades are major developments in semiconductor physics and technology. It has been possible to gain a fundamental understanding of the electronic and optical properties of semiconductors on the basis of simple one-electron models, whereby the carriers of electricity are considered to be independent of each other and to interact with the ions and electrons in the solid through an effective periodic potential. For many important applications, the effect of this periodic potential is to endow the electronic carriers of electricity with an effective mass which differs from the free electron mass and describes the acceleration of this charge carrier in the solid by an applied electric field. From the technological side, the major advances have been the discovery of the transistor and its miniaturization, as well as the development of electronic devices based on the transistor and transistor circuits. Of particular importance has been the incorporation of many of these tiny transistors into electronic circuits, called integrated circuits, which are so small in size that they can reside within a single silicon chip that can fit on the head of a pin! This development of integrated circuit technology has revolutionized the computer industry and has made available small, cheap, and reliable computers (e.g., the hand calculator). It will yet be some time before the present massive computerization development matures and its impact is fully appreciated in our daily lives.

The discovery and development of the maser (microwave amplification by stimulated emission of radiation) and the laser (the analogous device at optical frequencies) during the 1950s and 1960s marks a second major breakthrough which occurred in the post-World War II era. These developments have ushered in the new and active field of quantum electronics. The laser provides a coherent, highly collimated, spectrally pure light source which can be operated either on a continuous basis (cw) or on a pulsed basis. As sources of cw electromagnetic radiation, lasers have provided frequency standards with much higher spectral purity and long-term frequency stability than had been previously envisaged. When operated on a pulsed basis, lasers can deliver enormously high output power. The advent of very high power laser sources opened up the field of nonlinear optics and has led to many important applications in the mixing of optical frequencies to generate both ultraviolet and far infrared coherent radiation. Some of the more common practical applications of lasers are in welding and joining metals, in surveying for highway construction, in surgery for the repair of detached retinas, and very recently for the development of advanced techniques for isotope separation. Lasers are attractive for communication applications because of the enormous number of available communication channels at optical carrier frequencies. With the recent development of very low loss optical fibers, advanced research programs are now under way in the new field of integrated optics to develop the miniaturized optical components necessary for communication at optical frequencies.

Superconductivity is one of the truly remarkable properties of solids, whereby some metals below a characteristic critical temperature can conduct electricity without dissipation. Although first identified in 1911, practical superconductivity devices were not made until the late 1950s with the development of superconducting magnets and coinciding with a microscopic explanation of the phenomenon of superconductivity. The widespread availability of superconducting magnets has greatly stimulated research at high magnetic fields and is now finding application to the electrical power generation industry. Miniature superconducting devices are also important for the measurement of tiny electrical voltages and for possible switching applications in the computer industry.

Major advances in materials preparation, purification, and characterization and new developments in high vacuum technology have made possible a detailed study of surfaces. Surface science is one of the expanding fields of the 1970s which is today attracting the attention of interdisciplinary scientists and engineers.

Active fields in solid-state physics and engineering change from one decade to another, and so also do the career patterns of researchers in these fields. On looking back on my own career, I can see how I have moved from one field to another, having worked in superconductivity in the 1950s, in semiconductors and optics in the 1960s, and laser applications in the 1970s. Although we do not know where the new and active research areas will be in the future, we do believe that such areas will exist and that we will be able to find them.

"NO WIDER THAN THE HEART"

CELESTE ULRICH

University of North Carolina—Greensboro

LIKE MANY LITTLE girls, I loved activity. Walking seemed to suggest senility, so I ran, hopped, jumped, skipped, and somersaulted my way into adolescence. Growing up in a neighborhood where there were only boys fostered my activity desires, and I climbed trees, jumped off garage roofs, tackled quarterbacks, built shacks, and took my turn on the monkeyvine with my brother and his friends. It never occurred to me that there was anything unnatural about my insatiable lust to move. My young parents, who were both employed, seemed satisfied with my life style and I loved bouncing from one situation to another.

Like many little girls, I sought some sort of identity. The people who participated in all of the things that I cared for were male. Because I was a "real sport," my dad used to brag to his friends, "She is as good as any boy." Like Peppermint Patty, I was his "rare gem." I knew that being a boy was a "good" thing: it meant that you were brave, strong, enduring, adventurous, daring, and forceful, and I liked being like that. But I also knew that I wasn't a boy; I was "just as good as any boy."

My mother was one of my role models, and I kept watching her to see how she handled things. She was young, vibrant, tenacious, and she went to work every day. In addition, she managed a household and still had time and energy to kiss skinned knees and make hair bows. I knew that she wasn't like "other mothers" and every once in a while I would wish that she would look older and more staid, more like my grandmother. Other children's mothers looked like my grandmother! But Mom seemed to be able to do many things. I liked that.

My other female models were my teachers. For the most part they were dedicated and concerned women who were sure that education was the key to a better life. They approved of my persistent curiosity and kept encouraging me to do more things and find out more about my world. In my elementary school, if you finished your reading or arithmetic lessons before the rest of the group, you were allowed to go to the window sill and take an extra packet of what was called "seat work." "Seat work" was game-oriented readings and computations. You learned to reason, to be logical in your reasoning, and to keep pushing yourself to take the next step. If you were able to fathom your "seat work" packet, and it was "correct," the teacher put a small blue star next to your name. Ten blue stars earned a gold star, a big gold star. I liked gold stars. I liked being smart and getting to do "seat work," and being asked to erase the blackboards because I was finished before the rest. Being a girl in school seemed to be a good thing. The teachers were always complaining about the boys—especially the boys' conduct—and I sensed that the smart boys were having a hard time with their gang. But teachers expected little girls to be good students. I fulfilled their expectations and adopted their expectations as my own.

As a child, it seemed to me that I had the best of two worlds. In activity events, I was "as good as any boy," and in school I was "just what we would expect of her." I remember wishing that a few of my bubble gum "shooting cards" would have Alice Marble, Helen Moody, or the "Babe" on them, but I reasoned that women really were not of the calibre of Lou Gehrig, Ben Hogan, and Slingin' Sammy Baugh. I wrote compositions on "Emiline Pankhurst—Leader of Destiny," "The Woman Who Won the West—Sakachawea" and "Marie Curie—Female Scientist." I did not know that I was a feminist or that I had already made decisions about my life interests. I was just a little girl who was enjoying a "Pippa passing" childhood.

As adolescence approached, I began to find different attitudes about my patterns of behavior. My parents seemed concerned that I was still "rough-housing" with the boys, and I can remember my Dad saying to my mother, "Can't you get her out of those shorts and blue jeans and into dresses?" Maybe I was no longer his rare gem! I can remember the junior high school principal bemoaning the fact that the top five honor students were all girls. I can remember being told that the Boys' Leaders Club would be advised by the principal and that he would try to find somebody who would "take" the Girls' Leaders Club. I remember being told by the god-like Adonis who was known as "Coach" that girls didn't need basketball uniforms, warm-up suits, and an activity bus for their games because it was all "just for fun." I began to really understand that girls were not so important as boys and that we were not to have advantages in education unless we were better than boys. It wasn't an awful shock—it seemed natural. Although I chafed at the inequities and wished for a better day which suggested egalitarianism, I was happy and overtly content in my acceptance of the inevitable.

One of the few places in education where I saw women having some chance to function without always catering to male demands was in the gymnasium. There was a woman physical education teacher, a girls' gymnasium, and a female athletic association. It seemed to me like a panacea for all of my covert concerns. In physical education classes your teachers expected to see you in shorts and slacks, you could participate in all of the activity you wished, and they were supportive. In addition, they encouraged scholarship, suggesting that sport activity and good grades were an expected positive correlation. I liked their informality, their caring concern, their autonomy with regard to program, and their belief in the female of the species. My alliance with physical education seemed to be a natural. It was both an escape and an opportunity. I started to program myself so that I could become a physical educator.

It looked like a brave new world for me—a combination of activity and scholarship, association with people who believed in women and their potential, and the opportunity to be oneself. It was exciting, and I basked in Millay's world view:

> "All I could see from where I stood was three long mountains and a wood; I turned and looked another way and saw three islands in a bay—over these things I could not see: these were things that bounded me."

But it seemed enough—"I could touch them with my hand, almost, I thought, from where I stand!" Ahead loomed scholarship, activity, and the chance to serve. Ahead loomed physical education.

INDEPENDENCE AND SELF-DETERMINATION

Like many young women, I was excited about college. It was a different way of life, with the opportunity for independence and self determination. I put aside my apprehensions about being a bit different. The fact that I enjoyed playing field hockey instead of being a cheerleader seemed reasonable, and I was sure that the highly intellectual college community would understand that a person was a whole being and not a dichotomy of mind and body.

But I was to have a rude awakening to the prudish, snobbish, elitist academic life. It started with my female professors, who suggested that since I was an able student, there seemed to be "no reason" why I would "have" to choose physical education as a major. They urged me to turn to biology, sociology, psychology, or languages, assuring me that I had the ability to conquer those Olympian peaks of the intellect. The more conservative sneered at the entire area of physical education, and the more liberal kept assuring me that there would be plenty of time in my life "to play games," that I should take advantage of education while it was available, education being equated with the arts and sciences. I looked at my schedule and saw courses entitled biology, chemistry, physiology, physics, Shakespeare, music, French, psychology, philosophy, sociology, political science, history, and mathematics listed, and it appeared to me that I *was* taking advantage of my educational opportunities. But somehow, I felt that my course work was not quite legitimate in academic eyes; I contracted for additional hours in biology and sociology to gain academic respectability and approval from my mentors.

I also began to feel different as I heard snide remarks about the suggested life-styles of female educators. These came mostly from my male instructors, who talked about tom-boyishness, masculine walks, superstars, and hints about lesbianism. In that era, when the topic of homosexuality was not even included in sociology texts, I was at a loss as to their implications, and I kept wondering what they saw that I did not see. The women with whom I worked seemed quite normal in all respects. They were forceful, driving, enduring, powerful, assertive women—"as good as any man."

I was not altogether comfortable with the displeasure of the males, a displeasure which extended to the men whom I dated and even to some members of my own family. They kept suggesting that I would "outgrow" my disposition toward activity, I would mature beyond sport, and I would be willing to accept the decorum, dignity, and poise which were my assigned birthright as a female.

I am not sure to this day whether it was because of a stubborn streak which made me want to prove myself, or whether I was already committed to the idea that a woman can be anything she wants to be. But for some reason, I chose to ignore the sage advice of my friends and examplars and continued to prepare myself in the area of knowledge known as physical education. I acquiesced to their admonitions by making sure that I looked like a "lady" (heels, hose, hats, gloves, and girdles), and acted like a "lady" (don't rock the boat, be supportive of male endeavors and never, absolutely never, beat a man in tennis). As a reasonably good tennis player, the last admonition tended to stick in my craw, but I realized the wisdom of the admonition and tried to avoid playing men whom I believed I might beat.

Since I was in undergraduate school during World War II, it tended to be a woman's world in academe. True we were all "supporting the men at the front" and writing long, involved love letters to THE man of the hour, never knowing whether he would be alive to read our declarations; but we were also making our own decisions, learning that Rosie the Riveter was a capable human being, and running the show without our intended mates. It was a heady and sobering experience. You liked being in charge, you found out that the world "out there" wasn't as frightening as it was exciting, you felt that there was chance to do something important and meaningful for all people instead of just a small, intimate group. On the other hand, you were holding it all together until the men came home, you were anticipating the luxury of shared decision-making, you were haunted by a population depleted of males, especially depleted of *your* males.

Like a number of young women in the 1940s, I decided to go to graduate school until such time as I could get everything sorted out. The war was over, and the men were home. Graduate schools were crowded with hollow-eyed, young men, sage beyond their years. What you had been doing during the war years suddenly seemed unimportant as you heard of the Bulge, the Slot, Dachau, Anzio, Tokyo Rose, and Anola Gay. It was good to have the men with you, but they were ambitious and driving, and their five-year interlude had given them focus, force and direction. You found that you were interacting with a group of men who did not understand what had happened to you while they were away and wanted to "get on with it" as fast as they could so as to catch up with lost time. They had no desire for the social amenities between males and females, and they were more than a bit irritated that something had happened to the women while they were gone. Women had become demanding and assertive and abrasive, and things were not as they used to be.

My reactions to the war veterans ranged from compassion and reverence to hatred and envy. I thought that they were different, and I resented the fact that many of them were attempting to put me in my place. I didn't have a place, and I was not to be manipulated into some niche which I had had no part in creating. Besides, that motivational worm which lurks in the heart of many of us had been feeding openly and amply in me and its appetite was not to be satisfied. I had learned how to seek success, I had learned that the fear of failure was not an impossible obstacle, and I was determined to come to grips with a world which I had a part in creating.

In addition, the area of knowledge to which I was attentive was exploding with ideas. The teaching of sport skills was no longer the sole focus of physical education. The addiction to physical fitness was purged, and physical educators were at long last synthesizing their discrete disciplines into an interdisciplinary body which promised meaning as it was understood. I was upset and excited, upset because things were changing so rapidly that I was unsure of myself, and excited because the change was so volatile and relevant, it looked as if:

> "all at once things seemed so small my breath came short, and scarce at all . . . The sky, I thought, is not so grand; I most could touch it with my hand!"

INTO THE TEACHING ARENA

So, armed with a master's degree, with a surety about my knowledge, and with a wordless decision that I could "make it on my own," I jumped into the teaching arena. If I had been asked at that time, I am sure I could not have articulated that I had made a decision about my life, but I had. I had decided that unless some sort of fantastic young Lochinvar rode out of the west, a man who would be willing to really share a joint life, that marriage was not for me. I had been told by one young swain that he "could not live without me" and I found the encompassing possessiveness so restricting that I had run, not walked, to the nearest exit. It was frightening. In those days, a decision against marriage, even one not voiced, was a monumental decision; it suggested a world of anomie.

During the ten years that I taught as a young college instructor in the department of physical education, I learned many things. I had allied myself with a college designated for women, and there was a relatively high proportion of females on the professional staff—even some outside the departments of physical education and home economics! The upper echelon of administrators was entirely male, except for one female with the enticing title, "Dean of Women." I wondered why at an all-female institution she was not dubbed Dean of Students, but my inquiries were either ignored or considered challenging and threatening. My experience reinforced my ideas that women were intelligent, caring, supportive human beings, that life would never be what it was pre-World War II. I also knew that physical education was unique. As a discipline it was concerned with the holistic person and attentive to humanistic approaches to teaching-learning; it went beyond addressing itself to the sterile discriminative recall in areas of cognition which venerate an entity called "mind."

Those ten years were important because they led me to the threshold of action. I had been drifting along, doing a reasonably good job in teaching, learning a great deal about people and how they operated, and feeling that I had eons ahead of me in which to come to grips with myself and my world. But suddenly I was 32, and the world was turning just as rapidly as it did when I was 22, only I wasn't sure where in the spinning orbit I was. What had been a comfortable rut suddenly became an uncomfortable grave:

"and reaching up my hand to try, I screamed to feel it touch the sky
. . . Ah, awful weight! Infinity pressed down upon the finite Me!"

Something had to change and it became more and more apparent that the something would have to be me. Graduate work or foreign travel seemed to be escape hatches. I am not sure exactly what I was escaping from or to, but I believe it was an escape from a serenity which provided comfort but no promise to the adventure of the unknown. Fortunately for me, I had heard an erudite and challenging presentation at a professional convention by Dr. Eleanor Metheny, a former professor at the University of Southern California. I was interested in knowing whether she just spoke well or if she was good enough to sustain intellectual excitement on a day-in a day-out basis. I trekked across country to come to Los Angeles one summer and was more than satisfied with the experience that I had. I had zeroed in on a model personality which made lucid the interactions for which I had been looking. Here was an intelligent, forceful woman who saw value in the holistic approach to the teaching-learning situation and who was comfortable with herself. I do not mean to imply that Eleanor Metheny was a paragon of virtue—far from it, but she did project for me the symbol of possibility. She was intellectually astute, she wrote well, she handled ideas in a logical manner, she was not afraid to think in ways which were not popular. She herself was never apologetic for what she was or was not, never testing her mettle against others, only responsible to self and society. It was an unsettling, yet satisfying, enounter and I felt the

> "startled storm-clouds reared on high and plunged in terror down the sky!"

I had been struck with the bolt of belief—belief in self, my area of knowledge, the future of women, and my potential contribution to that interlaced design.

In retrospect, I believe that I had many people from whom I drew strength, people who helped me understand that the struggle to attain selfhood was a worthwhile struggle. In many ways, all of these people suddenly focused into a composite personage—a person who was human rather than divine, a person who had liabilities as well as assets, and, fortunately for me, a person who was willing to take the time, effort and belief to energize a neophyte so that a potential might be pursued.

I remember my struggle to convince a graduate faculty that a doctoral dissertation in stress theory was a worthwhile avenue to explore. I was convinced that psychological stressors caused physiological trauma, which in turn affected behavior. And what is more, I was convinced that sexual distinctions were invalid with regard to ability to handle stress. So, by measuring a specific red blood cell, an eosinophile, I was able to suggest that there was reason to doubt the general assumption that women were incapable of handling emotionally charged situations and hence should be banished to the croquet courts or tiddly-winks tables rather than participating in the blood and guts encounters of basketball, field hockey, tennis, badminton, and golf. It is hardly a startling find in today's world, but just twenty years ago there were people questioning my right to investigate a phenomenon which had the conventional acceptance of the medical and educational establishments: girls did not participate in highly competitive situations; they just couldn't handle that sort of stress.

My "discovery" was considerably below the impact of that of Semmelweis', but it met with about as much disdain. It was a known fact that males and females were different, and that meant that they were to be treated differently with regard to sport situations. Empirical evidence and actual experience belied what the textbooks told us about women's ability, but we were too enculturated to change the patterns of sport performance. In our society, even bicycles have a gender!

With a new diploma tucked under my arm and the right to add Ph.D. to my name, if I wished, I was reasonably sure that I had reached a goal. However, the goal was a mere oasis in the desert trek towards self-actualization and social responsibility. Articles, speeches, and consulting services now all had to be programmed into a busy teaching life.

The additional research to further test hypotheses was the easiest part of all my self-imposed assignments. Experimental research using a statistical tool is the simplest of all educational ventures. I keep wondering why promotion committees at institutions of higher learning are so enamored of such an elementary form of erudition. Admittedly, finding a hypothesis and concocting the research design are demanding tasks, but after that it's all downhill. To be sure, the collection of data, especially when you are using human subjects, is frustrating and laborious, and the analysis and the interpretation of the data are tedious processes. But experimental research has an accepted format, demands little innovative thinking, and is subject to rather objective and expeditious verification. The production of such articles for refereed research journals involves time and commitment, but it is an easy assignment to thwart "publish or perish" demands.

PLAY AND HUMAN MOVEMENT

Much harder is the attempt to synthesize existing information into some sort of a conceptual model which can provide a paradigm for further exploration. In physical education, both human movement and the social institution of sport have the potential of providing salient paradigms which will enhance understandings about human movement phenomena utilized in play behaviors which will result in functional integrity. For that is what physical education is all about—the art and science of human movement, with special attention to play behaviors. Now, to attempt to synthesize all of the tidbits of knowledge which deal with play and human movement is a gargantuan task; understanding the laws of nuclear physics is child's play compared to understanding child's play.

My own personal attempts at synthesizing ideas have been tantalizing and demanding. They have not been satisfying and fulfilling. No sooner have you concocted one model than you see its structural weakness, and revision utimately leads to destruction. Models are very difficult to alter without losing their integrity. The work that Metheny and Elfeldt did with regard to the meaning of movement is a classic example of an initial paradigm which sponsored subsequent understandings about the shape, form and perception of movement experiences. The model projected by John Nixon and me for the body of knowledge of physical education is still in the process of being tested; already severe flaws have been noted.

The paradigm for play behavior suggested by Huizinga and the paradigm regarding games concocted by Callois have already altered interpretations of human behavior and are of great influence with regard to research centered about sport phenomena.

The most difficult of all intellectual assignments is the creation of unique knowledge. Writers of books which are *not* heavily footnoted are the ones to be admired. That means that the individual has pulled knowledge out of self, has concocted knowledge. Such a task requires a discipline of self which is unreal. On those occasions when whatever I am doing has to come entirely from me, I am fatigued before I begin . . . I get tired just thinking about what I must do. For myself, I have to be in certain places: I do not think creatively in my office at school—I am too surrounded by the nitty-gritty of practical operations. I have to have a hunk of time, the right place, reasonable organization in terms of my expectations, and the willingness to sit for long periods at a desk when nothing seems to be happening. When you create, you first must structure chaos, and then you attempt to find your way out of that labyrinth of ideas. There are phases when the going is really difficult. I keep positively reinforcing myself as I go along. If I accomplish a set goal, I let myself fix a cup of coffee; if I translate an idea into reasonably lucid words, I am entitled to a walk from the den to the side of the porch and back; if I gain a new insight, I am allowed to answer the next telephone call rather than ignore it. It is a childish way to force oneself to create, and I have great admiration and respect for those who can sit themselves in front of a typewriter and invent ideas for four hours a day and then fold up their tents and silently steal away. For myself, the creation of ideas is very hard work; I am seldom satisfied with the results, because I never seem to be finished. One idea keeps leading to another.

Sometimes, for diversion, those of us in education take off from the exacting tasks of thinking and slosh about in the puddles of organizational leadership. When you assume leadership roles, you have the task of attempting to implement the ideas of other people; your own concepts often must take a back seat. However, designing the patterns of human interaction is "heady stuff," especially when you realize how close are the manipulator and the enabler. There are times in leadership when you feel as if you are seated at a gigantic organ made up of people and, if you only have the wisdom to play the right keys, you may be able to create a harmony of tones which will add distinction to the operation and will expand the dimension of each contributor. Working in higher education and specifically in physical education, I have had numerous opportunities to play such an organ, and to be played upon by others who have been leaders. You have to be careful, because such an operation can be so attractive that you are charmed by your musical ability, and you can forget about your responsibility to provide hard-core material for the cutting edge of your disciplinary adventure.

However, while I am talking about leadership roles, let me talk just a bit about the ecstasy of human interaction when it is devoid of gender connotations. My professional organization, the American Alliance for Health, Physical Education, and Recreation has alternated leadership by sex since 1932. In addition, governance has always been bisexual. Until you have had a professional asexual experience in a real-life situation, you cannot know the pure joy of being accepted for your ideas and your contributions without implications regarding sexual bias. Sometimes you can have a simulation of that experience when you are with an all-woman's group, and I assume that the same is true for all-male groups. But the asexual experience in a group which is sexually integrated is an opportunity worth pursuing. It is like doubling up on your assets without accruing liabilities.

As a mature professional person, I see many options ahead of me. The area of physical education is on the verge of a great breakthrough. We are exploring the motoric experience in ways which hold promise for human understanding. We are willing to commit ourselves to the body as "the radical root of reality" and are now suggesting that body is no longer a temple to house the self, but instead that body is self. We are an integral part of the education matrix, and I believe we are making a unique contribution to humanistic understandings as well as exploring behavioristic methods which suggest that humans can be programmed to realize their potentials. Best of all, I believe that we are going to provide the leadership for ameliorating conditions regarding sexism in the schools. As the only gender-identified subject matter in the entire educational system, we have been prime examples of sexism at its worst and at its best. As physical educators put it all together and provide for individuals the opportunities to be whatever it is they wish to be, the walls of sexism will crumble to the blast of Gabriel's physical education trumpet.

I am a woman who has had opportunities in higher education. Some of those opportunities have been available because I was in a field which legislated sexual identity and insisted upon quota systems for females long before the federal government ever thought of the idea. Some of the opportunities have come about because I have had female administrators who did not cater to the "old school tie" and were not beholden to the lockerroom boys. Some of the opportunities have come about because I was a part of a generational mutation which entertained change even when we did not understand it and welcomed it long before we knew how to control it. Some of the opportunities came about because I had all of the right credentials and there were no men to promote over me, so there just wasn't any reason why I shouldn't progress as anticipated. Some of the opportunities came about because, like many other little girls, I liked activity and scholarship and learned to combine the two behaviors.

Lots of things will happen over the next decade, things which people like yourselves will bring to fruition. We will not be in Erehwon in the next

decade, for we will be employing forensic guidelines and dialectic inter-
faces to realize our potential as women. Those of us who have achieved a
degree of success will delight in the renascence of human spirit being
sponsored by young people who are honestly committed to the betterment
of the human condition. Physical educators are willing to pledge their
support to such a noble cause.

There is a rich and exciting world to explore, a world which suggests
that women, activity, and scholarship are correlating factors in the process
of self-actualization.

"The world stands out on either side, no wider than the heart is
wide, and up above the world, the sky, no higher than the soul is
high."

In our wide world and high sky you and I will need faith, stamina,
courage and tenacity. Friends, colleagues—be of good heart!

ANTHROPOLOGICAL CHARTING OF THE FRONTIER

LAURA NADER

University of California, Berkeley

IN RECONSTRUCTING MY intellectual history, several big and little events come to mind. Most of these events involved a conflict of ideas and triggered new directions in research. Throughout my educational career I carried points of view that usually clashed enough with the general ideas around me as to make me feel different. While feeling different was not always comfortable, the contradictions that I experienced always helped to sharpen questions of value which underlie the directions I have explored in anthropology.

As a senior in an Eastern girl's school, I majored in romance languages. I wrote an honors thesis, "The Concept of Leadership in Mexican Revolutionary Novels." While such an endeavour might sound mundane enough today, in the early 1950s I was informed by the chairwoman of the department that what I had written was neither dealing literarily with literature, nor was it literature in any way; it was sociology, and as such she could not award me a degree in romance languages (even though the thesis happened also to be written in Spanish). In a rather dazed state I was sent to the sociology department where I was informed that while my thesis dealt with interesting sociological questions they could not award me my B.A. in sociology because I had never taken a course in sociology. The president of the college had to settle the matter by awarding me a degree in Latin-American Studies. In the process the president apologized for the rigidity of departments. Nevertheless, I left his office in bewilderment.

As a high school student I had no idea what I wanted to be. I had no idea of what I wanted to be even through college, nor did I know what I wanted to do, though I knew I wanted to do and be something. I wrote my story in a letter to my older brother, then an anthropology student at the University of Toronto. In answer he sent me a copy of Clyde Kluckhohn's book *Mirror for Man*. As I read this prize-winning book I remember saying to myself, "*I* am an anthropologist."

After graduation I spent a year working in New York as a typist and then as an "information analyst" at the Indonesian consulate. In the evenings I took courses in Spanish philosophy at Columbia University and also read anthropology. I then applied and was accepted to graduate school at Radcliffe College (Harvard University), where I intended to study anthropology at the Peabody Museum with Clyde Kluckhohn. But once again I was faced with the problem of choice. I now knew that I wanted to work as an anthropologist, but what did I want to study as an anthropologist? In this paper I will try to describe some of the factors that influenced my choice of what to study, whether and what to explore. As we shall see, my choice of what to study was generated by basic disciplinary values, by values relating to my individuality, to my sex, and in greater part as I grow older to happenings and events in the world around me. Whatever directions I chose, there were both constraining and supporting factors, some inside the profession and some outside.

When I entered graduate school I was self-conscious about being a student in anthropology, a subject I had never formally studied. I was unself-conscious prior to entry about being a woman graduate student. My own mother had been a teacher, and throughout our time as youngsters had regaled us with exciting stories of her teaching career in a large Lebanese village. Fieldwork as anthropology was simply to be the modern version of her career. However, my lack of self-consciousness was soon altered by the numerous stories about women graduate students that continually circulated at Harvard. Mostly myths, these stories dealt with the rates of survival of women graduates due to lack of commitment, possibility of marriage and children, and imposition of such decisions on professional dedication. Questions of intent and motivation were regularly directed at the women graduates, and there were few women models on the Harvard scene at the time: Dr. Beatrice Whiting was in a research capacity at the Institute of Human Development, and Dr. Cora DuBois was hired to fill a special chair at Radcliffe. I was worried of failure and the shame failure would bring; the fact of being a woman graduate meant that I had to try harder.

A PERIOD OF CONFORMITY

Graduate school is a place where students learn the professional values that guide how and what research is to be done. What is most interesting about the process of learning is that the most important values are learned as part of the daily routine without any particular ado, and without any particular questioning. One can be skeptical during graduate school about particular theories and findings, but rarely about the direction of the whole endeavor. Graduate school is where you learn the professional subculture. Those that refuse to conform usually leave to try their luck elsewhere.

The following unwritten rules could be identified as guiding us in our work: It is important to study non-Western cultures; ethnographic description is of value as a means to generalization; kinship is the most prestigious topic; new data and new theory are often stimulated by innovations in methods, and not vice-versa; knowledge of previous work is crucial to the development of ideas; anthropologists should "suffer" while in the field.

As a graduate student I wrote three papers, and, although none of these papers were of publishable quality, they were important to my intellectual and personal development. The topics were chosen by me with little direction as to how one decides what to work on except in following the widely accepted maxim: "Study what interests you." The papers reflected the anthropological concerns of the time as well as my reaction to the academic world as I saw it. One paper dealt rather abstractly with problems in the methodology of comparison and was written jointly with two male graduate students. The second paper was an ethnographic description of the Zapotec peoples in Mexico. The third paper was a comparative study which set about to question the validity of the American belief that "working women do not make 'good' mothers," a belief that implies that non-working mothers do make good mothers. I was neither married nor a mother at the time, but I must have had concerns about such questions then.

In this paper on mothers I contrasted three cultures: one where mothers do very little work and where their mothering "instincts" were not too well developed and where they had little interest in their children; a second culture where mothers worked very hard and were too exhausted to pay very much attention to their children; and a third where women lived with their husband's lineage, did work but not to the point of exhaustion and were devoted mothers to their children. I concluded that any correlation between good mothering and whether women worked or not was simplistic and probably wrong. Some years later Beatrice Whiting wrote an article which concluded that the most contented mothers were probably those who worked outside the home but only part-time.

While a graduate student I took a part-time job with Arthur D. Little to work on questions related to women's customary practices during menstruation. The client in this case was a business corporation that sold products to women that function as collectors of menstrual blood. The clients we dealt with were men who were interested in selling to women—both here and abroad. "I want an answer right now, not tomorrow, and if that answer has to come off the top of your head that's where I want it to come from," the gentleman said to me. His comment was in response to my discovery that there was nothing in the literature on the Latin-American woman, and my question was, would they consider funding some good research on the subject. The techniques used at Arthur D. Little were almost in direct opposition to those of the University. There was a sense of urgency as versus little sense of urgency in the academy. There was an idea that one should do with what there is instead of probing for "enough" data. There was a certain free style based on the knowledge that if one is guessing right something will work (e.g. product sales will go up). The University had a certain heaviness about it. The experience was refreshing and gave me some idea of how one could operate to learn outside the walls of academia. What I learned I have incorporated into my academic style, particularly my style for brainstorming. It encouraged me to do more with what I have here and now, rather than waiting until "all the data" are in. It also taught me as my courses in physical anthropology had not, of the intimate relation between culture and biology.

During my fieldwork I was led to ask questions about the life cycle of women. It was from asking about menstruation and dysmenorrhea that I became fully cognizant of the effects of life-style on such medical problems as dysmenorrhea. Research in the United States at the time was concerned with individual rather than cultural explanations of dysmenorrhea. The women that I was to study had no problem with menstrual pain—nobody, that is, but the school teacher. It was from interviewing in fieldwork about menopause that I began to suspect that hot-flashes, hormonal imbalances, etc. might well be related to stress in life-style. The Zapotec women I studied had no word for menopause. They only chuckled when I asked about how they felt during this period: it was a time for having sexual intercourse without worrying about having children.

The experience at Harvard also had its pluses. Harvard taught us to be self-reliant; we were essentially self-taught in developing perspectives and in formulating problems. The people who taught us inspired us; they were devoted researchers not teachers. When it came time for field research, I had to find my own funds and work out my own research design with some help from older graduate students. I sent two applications into the only two places that seemed to be supporting social anthropological fieldwork in Mexico: the Doherty Foundation and the Mexican government through the Institute for International Education in New York. In order to apply for monies, I had to know ahead what it was I was intending to do and why. I had to develop a theoretical perspective and the appropriate methods for the problem.

Mexico was attractive to me because I had spent my junior year with Smith College in that country. The Zapotec Indians interested me because they were known to be independent entrepreneurs and high in self-esteem. I had read most of what had been written about them and in my readings had come across an article by Oscar Schmieder, a University of

California geographer who had written about the settlement patterns and the geography of the Sierra Madre del Sur (1930), a mountain region of Oaxaca inhabited by Zapotec and Mixe Indians. He had mapped the area, and on this map there was a blank spot labeled the Rincon. Nobody— neither geographers, historians, archaeologists, linguists, or anthropologists—had reported on the area. I would go there and study settlement patterns as suggested by the Schmieder article. Settlement patterns was a topic that would have utility in an ever-crowding world.

In the Spring of 1957 I located in the Rincon Zapotec area with the help of some engineers from the Papaloapan Commission, a development agency with experts working in the area. I proceeded to study the consequences of settlement pattern for social organization. I found two villages, one compact and one dispersed. Both were villages of approximately the same population size: some kind of controlled comparison seemed possible. I set about my work as planned, only to be interrupted first by accusations of being a Protestant missionary, and then by sickness that was to leave its mark upon my first fieldwork (Nader, 1964).

It was an enormous task I had set for myself. To study one village was difficult enough, but to study two with as general a focus as settlement pattern meant that I had to know intimately the workings of religious, political, work, and family organization in both places. I was worried about validating what I was learning and about knowing the difference between idiosyncratic and patterned behavior. I needed an independent validation of some of my observations about people in their roles and in their interactions with others. I collected law cases.

When I returned to Cambridge, I analyzed the cases to see how much about the society could be inferred and how much would check out with hypotheses that resulted from observation. In the process, however, I became interested in what happened in courts for its own sake. Court behavior was highly patterned and apparently not completely open-ended as were other data I had been collecting. The court cases had boundaries that were at the time a relief to me, especially because the research on settlement was so broadly conceived.

Up to this point my fieldwork had developed around topics somewhat by accident, a chain of choices that followed from my first choice of research area and topic. The first choice grew out of the traditional value placed in anthropology on the importance of extending our knowledge of the range of diversity in human kind. What was not apparent to me at the time were the blanks that an anthropologist of another time might have given higher priority. For example, an anthropologist with more of an historical sense might have been curious about the role of the lumber companies in planning the development of the area. Such a topic would have fallen squarely within the domain of changing land-use patterns, and the external relations of the Zapotec with large companies. Strangely enough, my graduate training, although strong in the area of pre- and post-Conquest history, completely bypassed the concept of a more recent history which affected the people that anthropologists study.

I did not choose to explore the cultural context of the biological stages that women pass through; in fact, at the time I did not even think about what it meant to be a woman in the field (Golde, 1970). In analyzing my materials I did not include very much on the cultural and social organization of women, though the greater part of my information came from women informants and my notes have a great deal in them on the lives of women. I was caught in a male mind-set. The fact that I had paid so little attention to the effect of bigger companies and big government in the area indicates another kind of mind-set.

POWER BROKERS AND THE NATIONAL CONTEXT

The first field experience after my doctorate was short and problem-oriented. I spent slightly over six weeks doing fieldwork in Lebanon. My central question was straightforward. I had read in the Islamic literature about Islamic law. Since Islam was an urban religion, I asked, did Islamic law really ever filter into the villages of the Middle East? If so, how much, and in what way? Was there really a difference in the way villages of different religious sects settled conflicts, or was there an indigenous "pre-Islamic" culture that overrode any impact of religious law?

I worked in a small Shia Moslem village in South Lebanon, a village characterized by a dual division organizational pattern. I focused on case materials, on procedure, and essentially I found what I had suspected: that Islamic law had only a small role to play in a Shia Moslem village, that social structural variables, both in Lebanon and in Mexico, were greater deciding factors in forums of justice and in legal procedure than were the cultural factors. I also found that the fact I was a woman, contrary to popular belief, was an asset.

My published report on this summer's work was again comparative and oriented to hypothesis testing. My work was again published in English, not Arabic, although one of the essays resulting from this summer's work (Nader, 1965) "Communication Between Village and City in the Modern Middle East," was later translated in Syria and republished in Arabic. Initially, when I requested funding for this study, I specifically argued that work on village law was necessary for developing nations. Such research would help those using the concept of unified law to strengthen their national base. However, with no sophisticated knowledge of national law, I was not at the time able to make any connection between my findings and national development questions, although some fourteen years later a student working with me at Berkeley did exactly that (Witty, 1975). From my work I had learned that forms of conflict resolution reflect a range of ward-heeling tactics whereby urban power brokers interact with villagers in trouble. While studying Shias, I found myself unable to ignore questions of power and nation, and this was made all the more likely because I was staying in the home of an urban power broker. Not only had social scientists studied men to the exclusion of women (see Epstein in this volume), but anthropologists had regularly studied the rural without understanding their relations to the powerful urban rich. In the years that followed I was to become painfully aware that anthropologists, myself included, were caught in a mind-set whereby we were trained to relate (and therefore to study) down rather than up. This was to make me aware of the presence of professional biases which determine the frame within which our choices are made.

In 1963-64 I was a Fellow at the Center for Advanced Study in the Behavioral Sciences at Stanford. While there I developed two ideas for research proposals, both of which stemmed directly from my graduate training. The experience provoked the further realization that the choice of what anthropologists study is not determined simply by professional values. I realized that as anthropologists we are subject to political power and the national context just as are the indigenes we study.

Of the two proposals submitted, one was a project which I called the Berkeley Village Law Project, and the second was a proposal to do a comparative study of groomprice which would be both behavioral and historical. The first project intended to train and send a team of graduate student researchers to various parts of the world on a descriptive and mapping mission in the hope that a homogeneously trained group could accomplish more than a set of unrelated researchers. They were to use an agreed-upon methodology and perspective to study the legal and extra-judicial systems of dispute settlement in villages. We are in the process of putting together a volume reflecting this effort in a book to be called *The Disputing Process.*

Again I intended to fill the descriptive gap and, more important, to supplement what I thought was a perspective that was too narrow to help us develop any clear understanding of the role of law *in* society because of the over-emphasis on understanding legal processes as to their systemic qualities, which may be seen as independent of the rest of society. I felt that the paucity of theoretical development in the field was due either to too micro or too macro a picture, and to the too few workers in this field. My approach was to study law behavior as part of a set of alternatives. In this application there was only an apology for any practical need to study such phenomenon: we need to know more about the disputing process in order to understand the etiology of conflict; new nations around the world were developing and integrating by means of the law, and I argued they could develop their national legal systems more sensibly if they knew what was already the working law of the land.

This proposal was sent to the National Institute of Mental Health and rejected for a variety of reasons, but one of the principal reasons, I was informed, was the youthful age of the principal investigator. I was in my early thirties at the time. We went ahead with the project anyway and supported the work piecemeal. Absence of general funding was not a deterrent, as individual support was then available at such places as the NIMH, but again I became aware of the national political context and the effects of "peer" review which affected what anthropologists would be supported by government to study. I have watched throughout the 1960s and the 1970s in particular how government agencies influence the choice of questions for research by such strategies as contract research or targeted research. Anthropologists have for the most part been reactive rather than proactive in their relations with government agencies, and we will shortly see some of the reasons for this defensive posture.

The second research proposal had a pure science intent with no apologies for applicability, and it was the most fun of the two proposals to write: Groomprice: Its Place in Cross-Cultural Investigation of Exchanges at Marriage. I was interested that the exchanges made at time of marriage seen on a global basis indicated that brideprice seemed to be associated with subsistence economies in which women participate, whereas dowry or groomprice were found in societies where the women have a lesser role in subsistence activities, in societies with a tendency towards patriliny, and with the concomitants of these patterns, urbanism and stratified society. Theories about marriage exchanges had raised more questions than they had answered about topics such as marriage stability and the distribution of property. With the help of the late Dr. Millicent Ayoub, we planned to ferret out the concomitants of groomprice through time and space. We had a modest proposal with clearcut goals and some neat hypotheses. It was a problem area which seemed ripe for theoretical breakthrough. We were funded by the National Science Foundation, a government organization which has traditionally supported scientific exploration rather than targeted research. Support for "pure" research places the burden of the ethical questions squarely on the shoulders of the research community receiving the support.

THE IMPACT OF THE SIXTIES

I returned from the Center to my University duties. I had just had a baby and would return to teaching in time to witness the beginnings of the Berkeley Free Speech Movement. The 1960s had a vital impact on the kinds of questions I was to ask in my research. So was the fact that I had three children during this decade. The impact was *not* one that made me decide to be more applied or more "relevant" and less pure science in approach. It did, however, make me ask different kinds of questions. It led me to challenge the popular notion that all things are equally important to study if you, the anthropologist, are interested in the subject. It led me to question the idea that dealing with contemporary issues somehow made one less objective, more biased, than if studying more distant societies. After all Durkheim and Weber had both made extraordinary contributions in theory and method from their study of the social problems and institutions of their day.

I had by the early or mid-sixties analyzed a good portion of my Zapotec data on law, and with the many legal questions being raised in the immediate context of that period I quite naturally began to ask questions bearing on the similarities and differences in the problem-solving functions of American and Zapotec law. I temporarily put aside my Zapotec data, for I found that the questions I asked my law colleagues were either greeted with puzzlement or by simple statements of "I don't know." The first questions I asked pertained to use patterns in the law. Who uses the American legal system and to what purpose? I found an absence of knowledge at every turn. No one seemed to know what citizens did with their legal problems when they did not have access to law. The alternatives to the American judicial system had not been studied. The more I searched, the more I realized that very little legal research had dealt with understanding the legal system as it in fact operates, and that the majority of legal writing existed as a dialogue between lawyers over matters pertaining to the interests of a practical profession.

The American and Zapotec legal situations were in striking contrast along three important dimensions: the purpose or function of courts, their availability for citizen use, and escalation patterns that eventually led people to resort to law. The American system seemed to be one where access to courts was difficult for people with everyday living problems. There was apparently little use of mechanisms for deescalating disputes as in the face-to-face societies that anthropologists had studied. For example, most major student incidents during the 1960s escalated to the police and courts without going through either student government or faculty government for hearing. Most often only university administrators heard the complaints, and, since it was usual that the complaint was directed against university administration, there was rarely a third party hearing until the situation was out of hand.

I decided to focus research attention on extra-judicial mechanisms for dispute settlement because (1) no one knew much about it, e.g., uncharted, (2) I thought that legal change would be more likely brought about by extra-judicial means, and (3) such a strategy would best allow for the development of theory on legal change. The consumers of law were not allowed access to a court that had sometime ago changed its function from an institution whose prime function was to solve disputes to an institution primarily concerned with facilitating economic transactions in American society.

I interested a few undergraduate students to look into a number of extra-judicial complaint hearing institutions, such as the Better Business Bureau, the California Insurance Commission, and the Bay Area pollution Agency. This work developed into the Berkeley Complaint Project. Again we found ourselves mapping in an area that was relatively unknown. Our survey and ethnographic studies of complaint management in state and federal offices, in voluntary organizations, in the media, in ward politics, in department stores, in unions, in corporate practice were often firsts. For the first time in my research there were policy questions: should the United States develop better complaint management systems and, if so, at what level—in the law, extra-legal, to meet individual needs, to stimulate structural change? There were also applied questions: how would we invent a system for complaint management that meets the various needs of people living in a democratic society? There were pure science questions: if we view the law as having systemic qualities, and the legal system as changing through time, what is it that explains the drift in a legal system?

Sr. Henry Maine (1861) described the change in Western law as a movement from status to contract. This change accompanied the evolution in society from kin-based to territorially-based groups. Equally important shifts accompanied industrialization and the mass production and sale of goods, whereby the majority of legal issues involve individuals with large-scale organizations, such as industry or government; whereby access to the legal system became most easily accessible to people of wealth; whereby employment patterns changed most people's self-employed status to that of employee. Our research on American law, a setting where access is limited due principally to cost and crowdedness and lack of knowledge, has led me to questions about the secondary consequences of no access to law such as objective and endemic powerlessness. What, we might ask, would Sir Henry Maine's conclusions have been had he concentrated on all the users and potential users of the legal system, rather than singling out for analysis legal specialists and the mechanisms available to them?

The 1960s were a time to rethink the academic disciplines. Anthropology students at Berkeley were asking for courses on the ethnography of elites. Law students were calling for courses on poverty and consumer law. I ventured to send two male anthropology students to Washington to study a powerful law firm—one of which was part of a small group of powerful law firms sometimes referred to as the fourth branch of government. The venture was unsuccessful. Colleagues attributed the failure to the lack of experience and training of the students; I attributed the failure to a certain set of mind which is found in the social sciences generally and which results in training students to "relate down rather than up." (Nader, 1972.)

The results of this experiment were unsettling in terms of what it is that determines what anthropologists study. Anthropologists have covered the globe studying the range of variation in human society, yet we were ignoring perhaps the most extreme form of society ever conceived, a society where a few people are able to control the lives of many by means of formal and "hidden" governments, by means of lawless uses of power. Yet my colleagues argued that studying a Washington law firm was not relevant to the training of an anthropologist.

It was not that anthropologists had not studied American society. Many had. It was that most of our studies had been of small groups, counterparts in small face-to-face societies—ethnicities, factories, neighborhoods. There were some exceptions, but in the main anthropologists had not studied vertical slices of American society (which would be the home version of cross-cultural), nor had we been concerned with power. Uncharted, and powerful, the elites must be studied. Nobody had studied the insurance industry, its social organization, its power networks, its impact on American culture. No one had studied the energy specialists and the national laboratories from whence they operate. No one had studied the advertising industry as the single most efficient socializing agent in American society. Little time had been spent on the multinational corporations—the nations within nations, the food industry that has managed to put most people in this country on a completely untested diet, a first in the history of people and a success story that should dazzle the dieticians. These areas of interest, it must be pointed out, raise no less serious scientific questions than do traditional studies of neighborhood groups. Then why, we might ask, is not more ethnographic woman- and manpower distributed to such topics? Is it that there are not enough anthropologists to go around? Is it inertia? Perhaps innovation is impossible, given certain types of professor-student relationships (Nader, n.d.).

To date the only sense of urgency shared by the whole profession is that related to the fact that certain peoples and cultures of the world might become extinct before they are recorded, and we have committed ourselves as a profession to study cultures before they become extinct. In the present case the argument for deployment of energy needs to be made in terms of studying ourselves before *we* are extinct. We live in a time when institutionalized insanity is endemic; few of us are studying this phenomenon. Why, when we have anthropologists who are studying the health states of individuals and cultures have we ignored the technologists and the technologists' research bases, places such as the Lawrence Berkeley Laboratory? Such institutions are impacting heavily upon our present and future social organization. Rare is the national laboratory with any social scientists on the staff. Rare it is that the human component is a consideration in planning large-scale technology. Yet no anthropologist or other social scientist has studied the nuclear accidents that have already occurred, nor have we studied the social and political consequences of nuclear technology before going full speed ahead. This is another kind of urgency, still related, however, to the question of biological and cultural extinction.

BEYOND THE DISCIPLINE

Anthropologists engage in public service to greater or lesser degrees while they are teaching in the university. I have during the past ten years engaged in much service work which has brought me in contact with a variety of professionals in many institutional contexts. Some of these professionals are academics and some, as with lawyers, are principally practitioners. As a result of the Berkeley Complaints Study and the reading of hundreds of citizen complaint letters, I have been in touch with the "thinking-of-the-people" about their life problems. What I choose to study and what I will train students to work on is less and less determined by traditional subject matter—a high priority when I was being trained, and more and more determined by the concerns of the world wider than academic anthropology. This is bound to happen to professionals who develop networks beyond their immediate professional ties: the stimuli are different.

For example, one of the realities in which academic anthropologists live today is not only that of a shrinking academic marketplace, but also that of shrinking research funds. Some years ago, while I was serving on the Cultural Anthropology Committee of the NIMH, I witnessed the virtual termination of support for pre-doctoral anthropology students and with it a blow to the predoctoral research that such training grants made possible. We participated in a variety of attempts to persuade the Institute to redistribute available funds to support more anthropological work. One such attempt was a conference on anthropological contributions to the understanding of mental health problems held at the Center for Advanced Study, Stanford, California. I cochaired this conference with R. Maretzki and also coedited the volume that resulted, *Cultural Illness and Health* (1973). In the introduction to that volume I noted the costs of paying attention to anthropological studies such as those we presented. Ethnography is uncomfortably revealing at times when studying American society, since the anthropologist is often studying the health system from the point of view of the client rather than from the point of view of the professional. Professionals do not like to be interfered with by "outsiders."

My experience in editing the *Cultural Illness* volume, coupled with observations made in the process of attending professional meetings with lawyers, doctors, chemists, physicists, engineers, etcetera, has stimulated new areas for ethnographic research relating to the belief patterns of professionals as they relate to specialized work performance. For example, a lawyer only "hears" that segment of a case which is law-related, and it follows that perhaps that process is missing from the handling of citizen problems by lawyers. Similarly, each type of child specialist looks at the different needs of the child. Territoriality, rather than cooperativeness, is strong in American professionalism. Horizontal rather than vertical integration is the rule: a doctor's reference group is other doctors and not her clients. What is interesting for the anthropologist is to develop an understanding of how professionals invent, feed on, and exacerbate many of America's so-called social problems, while others have a reverse impact. To study an engineer who says he is unable to discuss the question of safety "because it's built into the design," or the physicist who says he can't ask questions about the breeder reactor "because it is not my specialty," or the judge who can't understand his insurance policy—these are questions on the "frontiers of knowledge"—to understand the cognitive processes of experts.

It is a fascinating business finding out how in the development of professions we came to our present state. The science questions are there, along with the ethnographic data desperately needed for living. The anthropologists who teach civil servants "how to answer citizen requests in Americanese" will have many grateful citizens who will gladly pay for the research he or she is doing. The anthropologist who writes an ethnography of law for the Zapotecs will give them some historical perspective on their relations with the Mexican state and will be creating a new awareness in anthropology as well as among the Zapotec. These are questions that would not have occurred to me in my pre- or post-doctoral periods, and maybe they should not have. But the danger is that the questions that were top priority during one's graduate training become the questions we continue to work around as well-developed professionals, and if that is so, one is no longer on the "frontier."

A concluding example has influenced the questions I am pursuing. Since 1972 I have served on the Carnegie Council on Children. The Council is a mixed group of individuals from diverse disciplines, mostly representative of various parent perspectives on children, not, for the most part, professional child specialists. Our charge has been to map out the present state of childhood in America, to envisage a better world for children, and to develop mechanisms for improving our children's chances for a livable future. Our assessment of the present situation has been "uncovered" by every White House Commission on Children since the early part of this century: the richest country in the world cannot boast about the way it is caring for its children, feeding its children, about the health care, the educational advancements, the realization of potential for many of our children. It soon became clear in our study, also, that much of the research on children, since Freud, has focused on the intimate home environment in which children are brought up and within which they are said to develop. Most of our theories about how children are reared and the consequences of childrearing seek to explain the child as a product of family environment, rather than as a product of the wider social structure. As the Council meetings proceeded it became clear that, in as technologically complex a society as ours, parents are less and less the determining factors in the development of their children.

New questions should revolve around the professionals and the industries that are part of child rearing practices in America. Linkages must be made between the micro and the macro environments. We need studies about the role of insurance, the Social Security administration, and the real estate industry as they affect the childhood development of every person. We need to understand how corporate rotation schemes affect the children of executives and engineers. We need the documents which explain the effects on children of the ways banks and the real estate industry are segregating America. And we could add similar questions about the linkages between the obstetricians, the pediatricians, the teachers, and the Atomic Energy Commission—and the rearing of America's children. The important subject matter is not our children as isolates and not the Atomic Energy Commission or ERDA, but the often uncomfortable connections and linkages between them that will make us realize exactly *how* people in large-scale organizations are rearing our children— people that have the power and access to our children but rarely any of the responsibility. The recent kepone example in Hopewell, Virginia, is a direct case in point. A subsidiary of Allied Chemicals, Life Sciences, managed to create a situation whereby the workers in the plant, their families, and the waters and air of these parts of Virginia were affected by Allied Chemical policies, yet the writings of laws are such that true accountability, family-like accountability, will be unavailable to the victims.

NEW PRIORITIES

There are those of us who will remain unaffected by the world around us and who will continue to study in areas that are esoteric and related to scientific problems that have long been with us in anthropology—subjects such as Mayan hieroglyphics or the kinship system of the Australian aborigines. There are those of us who will choose to take old scientific questions into new domains, such as studying the cognitive form of professional biases or mind-sets, or who will study the variables which promote legal drift. There are those who will choose to emphasize the humanistic aspects of culture, who will interpret symbols and their meanings. We in anthropology are doing this in a planless sort of way, with no understanding or knowledge of how we are distributing our energies, and therefore, necessarily, no understanding of how we should distribute our efforts except through rarely voiced but deep prejudices that the best schools should concern themselves with the most esoteric work in the most ivory-tower manner (e.g. publishing articles written in specialized jargon in specialized scientific journals), whereas the Midwestern or southern schools can concern themselves with the real world (presumably because anything that might have policy implications is of lesser importance and should be studied at "lesser" schools), and the lesser people should also be the ones to communicate anthropological findings to the public. It was and is not always so in anthropology. Boas (Columbia University) was concerned with public questions; Clyde Kluckhohn (Harvard University) wrote a prize-winning book and the last such on anthropology for the layman (1949); Margaret Mead has always been concerned about the world she lives in.

How do we set priorities? A science that is simply satisfying the ego of individual scientists is doomed to repetitiveness and to knowing more about less and less. A statement that says something about progress in the field that makes it possible to solve new problems or aspects of old problems suggests a science that is cumulative in effort. A statement that tells us that the area on the map is blank may be in the process of redistributing womanpower in the profession. A statement that tells us that nobody has studied the insurance industry, although virtually every American life is touched by this industry, . . . such statements as these are on the frontiers of knowledge.

REFERENCES

Golde, P. (Ed.)
   1970 *Women in the Field.* Chicago: Aldine Press

Maine, Sir H. S.
   1861 *Ancient law.* London, John Murray. Paperback edition printed by Beacon Press, Boston, 1963.

Kluckhohn, C.
   1949 *Mirror for Man.* New York: Whittlesey House, McGraw-Hill Book Company.

Nader, L.
   1964 *Talea and Juquila: A Comparison of Zapotec Social Organization.* University of California Publications in American Archaeology and Ethnology, pp. 195-296, Vol. 48, No. 3.
   1965 "Communication between Village and City in the Modern Middle East," *Human Organization,* Special Issue: *Dimensions of Cultural Change in the Middle East,* John Gulick, Ed., pp. 18-24, Spring.
   1970 "From Anguish to Exultation," in *Women in the Field,* P. Golde, Ed., Aldine Press.
   1972 "Up the Anthropologist—perspectives gained from studying up," in *Reinventing Anthropology,* ed. D. Hymes, Pantheon Press.
   1973 (with T. Maretzki). *Cultural Illness and Health*—Essays in Human Adaptation. *Anthropological Studies,* no. 9.
   1974 Review of *A Childhood for Every Child*—the politics of parenthood, M. Gerzon. Harvard Educational Review, Fall.
   n.d. "Rejects and Role Models." Paper presented at the American Anthropological Association Meetings, San Francisco, 1975.

LAURA NADER

Schmieder, O.

1930 "The Settlements of the Tzapotec and Mije Indians," *University of California Publications in Geography,* IV Berkeley.

Whiting, B. Personal Communication.

Witty, C. J.

1975 *The Struggle for Progress:* the socio-political realities of legal pluralism. Ph.D. dissertation University of California, Berkeley.

FEMINISM AND THE EDUCATION OF WOMEN

FLORENCE HOWE

State University of New York,

College at Old Westbury

WHEN I WAS a student, my least favorite course was history. I had not learned to ask two or three questions which might have made a difference: *why? who made that decision? and what were women doing?* Indeed, I accepted history as given—a bland series of causes and results of wars. Even revolutions were uninteresting, the Civil War without human content, and the terms of U.S. presidents undistinguishable except for Washington, Lincoln, and the current (second) Roosevelt. I am not exaggerating. Though history repeated itself several times in the course of my education in New York City's public schools and Hunter College, I went off to graduate school without the slightest interest either in U.S. history or literature, and for the next four years I read British literature and as little British history as I could manage. It never occurred to me that people wrote history, ordinary people, as well as extraordinary ones. It never occurred to me that women were part of history or that they might write the story of their lives.

During my first year in graduate school, at Smith College, I chose to study Chaucer and Shakespeare, and to write my Master's thesis on Jonathan Swift's poetry, especially those poems addressed to or about women. Twenty-five years ago when I made that choice I was not a feminist, nor could I ask any questions of history. Though I chose to write about Swift's poems on women, my thesis projected one message only: Swift was an underestimated poet: indeed, I urged that he was a fine poet. Somehow, I had become his admirer and defender. My thesis explicated his poems, pointing to their well-constructed rhymes and rhythms, and urging the cleverness of their content, and even on occasion the appropriate wisdom of their views as expressed formally (aesthetically) by the poem. Never did I question the status of women in the eighteenth century, or seek information about the comparative privileges allotted to women and men; never did I attempt to evaluate Swift's views of women as compared with those of other men. And while I had read other eighteenth century *men* of letters on women—it would have been difficult to avoid the *Spectator* and *Tattler* or Pope's Belinda or Dr. Johnson's view of a woman preacher—never did I consider searching for the writings of *women* of letters on that subject or any other.

I tell this story in order to make clear the difference between then and now, not only in my own life but in the lives of students generally. Then I was a "new critic," reading poems to make sense of their design as aesthetic objects. It was a game that even I, a woman, could learn the rules of, gain practice in, and succeed in imitating the patterns for—patterns which had been laid out for me by others. Today I am a practicing historian, even, or should I say especially, when I read literature. Now I ask those hard questions with which I began: *why?* Why did Swift choose to write many poems—but not his major prose works—about women? *Who made that decision?* Who decided that women and men were to study Swift and Burke and Rousseau and *not* Mary Wollstonecraft? de Tocqueville and not Harriet Martineau? Benjamin Franklin and not Elizabeth Cady Stanton? *And what were women doing in the eighteenth century, and in other periods as well?* Why were women not part of the curriculum offered to me twenty-five and more years ago? Were women ever part of a curriculum? What might happen if, beginning now, women were to become part of the curriculum?

For the past ten years, I have been asking these questions; and this past year I have had a special opportunity to search for some answers.[1] My search has taken me to the archives of colleges and universities where I have been reading printed materials and manuscripts few or no people have viewed since they were first written or published. These are not secret documents; they have simply not been considered interesting. Before I describe what I have been finding in the fascinating catalogues, presidents' reports, minutes of Boards of Trustees and Regents, committee minutes and reports, student publications, student notebooks, faculty syllabi, correspondence, journals, and other documents, I want to make certain that we understand the questions with which I began.

THE PROCESS OF ACQUIRING QUESTIONS

The questions are at once both simple and complex. On one level, they involve the whole of knowledge: how do we *know* anything? who decides what is true? who decides that we should study this or that? Also the questions involve conceptions of the use or function of knowledge, and hence of power: of what use is knowing this or that? what power does knowledge maintain? whose power? On a simpler level, the questions can be focused in order to pursue research in archives: what education was offered to women in colleges and universities? with what promises of function? Put another way, what reasons were given for educating women and for what purpose was that education to fit them? Listed this way, my questions seem impossibly abstract, I know. Moreover, if you are interested, as I am, in the process of acquiring more questions, the listing may not be helpful. I shall return to the questions later; but first I want to describe the process of reaching them.

Before one can ask questions, one needs a frame of reference and consciousness about the existence of the frame. Some people call this frame of reference philosophy; others, an ideology. Allow me to illustrate.

Frames of reference come in many sizes, from very narrow to broad conceptions like those of Marx or Jung. One can also choose a focus for a frame of reference: one can apply Freudian or Marxist conceptions to art, for example, or to the whole growth of civilization. You remember that I said that in writing my Master's thesis I was practicing to be a "new critic." My frame of reference, therefore, included the conception of literature as being divisible into "good" and "bad" or "defective." As I state it, it sounds trivial, and I do not mean simply to trivialize that activity, though, when I think back to the period during which I was trying to write that thesis, I can remember feeling that I was groping desperately in the dark, feeling unconvinced and unconvincing about what I was doing. I did not understand then that critical judgments are more often a question of contemporary consciousness and experience than of anything else—and of broader frames of reference than the narrow one I knew. I had no sense of how much the judgments, even of individual critics, change in their own lifetimes: and even though I was a student of literature, I had not been taught that critical opinion had changed through the ages on the value of many individual writers, including, for example, Jonathan Swift. I had no basis, moreover, either in experience or consciousness on which to make my own judgments. Nor did I see my activity as one that might prepare me for teaching students how to make their own judgments. (After all, the study of literature in schools and colleges might be perceived as useful if it helped us make sense of our judgments, since we are all critics in our private lives, judging films, music, painting, even books that we see, listen to, look at, or read. But, of course, we must learn to ask *why?* and *who made that decision? and what were women doing?*)

It was not simply my youth, for people today as young as I was then are writing quite differently. Let me tell you about two papers that happen to have crossed my path. One appeared recently in a quarterly published by the University of Michigan's Women's Studies Program. "A Feminist Critique of *Measure for Measure*" takes to task not only Shakespeare's critics but the master himself. "As much as the critics irritated me," Patsy Schweickert writes, "their apprehension of the play is far from groundless."[2] Shakespeare "simply has not risen above his culture" with respect to the characterization of Isabella as sister, novitiate, and woman. Schweickert's daring essay, like much in feminist literary criticism, raises more questions than anyone can now answer—few of which my generation is even now prepared for.

A second example is an undergraduate honors thesis I recently received from Mary Kathryn Jewett, a graduating senior at Emory & Henry College in Virginia. Titled *Separate and Unequal: A Case History of Women at Martha Washington College and Emory & Henry College,* it is a lively, interesting, and well-documented account of more than 100 years of coordinate and then coeducation at her own institution. Looking carefully at policies and prognostications, Kathy Jewett contributes generously to the history of higher education for women. Yes, she *has written* history.

Both these young people are part of a large group of humanist feminist scholars now engaged in re-evaluating art, including literature, and reenvisioning and rewriting history. It is a massive task, for it requires that we look again or for the first time at the formerly invisible half of humankind—women of all races, classes, religions, and ethnic origins. It is a complex task because it is not merely a story of subjection and sacrifice, but one of survival, heroism, leadership, and struggle for change.

Feminist scholars today are saying that women's history, achievement, and future are important enough to be studied, described, analyzed, reported, worked for. A philosophical feminist says, "I care about women, and I believe that their history and ideas are important to all of us." When I call myself an ideological feminist, I am adding something to the philosopher's position: I am saying that I will put my research at the service of changing the status and conceptions of women. Indeed, my research project exists because I have very real questions about where women's education is going, where it should go, and how it should get there. I am interested in history because I hope that it will shed some light on the present and into the future. I want to understand not only how we got into some of our current predicaments but how we might proceed from here.

The questions I began my research with have grown out of a decade of discovering that the curriculum I had been taught, and the one I was passing on to my students, was male-centered and male-biased. White middle-class male-centered and male-biased. Countless studies and other kinds of analysis now exist to demonstrate the cultural sexist bias of the curriculum, and I won't bore you by reviewing that material here.[3] But I should like to make clear that when I was in college or graduate school, I never once heard the names of Elizabeth Cady Stanton or Susan B. Anthony, much less studied their writings and achievements. I had not read Simone de Beauvoir until 1965, when I was also reading Betty Friedan and Doris Lessing. For me, and for other feminists of my generation and for those younger as well, Kate Millett's *Sexual Politics,* now five years old, was the ultimate "awakening." For people like me who need information as well as experience, Millett was, like de Beauvoir and Friedan, compelling.

LOST MASTERPIECES REGAINED

Because of those books and others that I was reading even as I was trying to teach women students about their histories and to move them to talk about their lives, hopes, and desires, I began to realize that if we were to change the education of women, to provide them with the history and role models they needed, we would have to write new materials or republish those that had been lost. As some of you know, The Feminist Press was born during this period, some five years ago, and at the end of its first year, Tillie Olsen offered our first lost treasure, *Life in the Iron Mills* by Rebecca Harding Davis. I mention this work because it is an admitted masterpiece, lost to us from its first date of publication in 1861, and hence until this time never part of the curriculum. If Davis had been lost, we speculated, how many others were there? That question began to haunt me, as The Feminist Press began to publish other lost American women writers: Charlotte Perkins Gilman, Agnes Smedley, Kate Chopin, and Mary Wilkins Freeman. Why had they been lost? Who had "lost" them?

I began to wonder, what if I had read these writers when I was young? how might I have turned out? And then other possibilities occurred: perhaps they hadn't been lost originally at all? perhaps it's the history of these writers that's been lost? perhaps young people, at some moment in time, had read these lost women writers? perhaps, I speculated, young women in college late in the nineteenth century had read feminist fiction writers and other feminist prose writers as well, perhaps they had also studied, as part of their history courses, the history of efforts to gain suffrage?

And perhaps you are beginning to see how I got from my dissatisfaction with the male-centered curriculum and my desire for a more balanced and inclusive curriculum to wanting to know whether there had ever been anything different. I need to add to this process one other factor. In the six years since the women's movement touched the campus, an educational phenomenon known as women's studies had developed in nearly 1,000 colleges and universities, offering more than 5,000 courses and 125 programs, half of them degree-granting or minor-offering.[4] I added to my list of questions about the history of the curriculum others concerning the future of women's studies: should women's studies courses and programs be developed into separate departments with their own faculties, budgets, majors? what *is* the future of women's studies? what is the best way to design a curriculum that reflects and is immediately responsive to the explosion of knowledge created by the academic arm of the women's movement?

What have I found? What conclusions have I reached? My research has made clear to me three phases of feminism—we are now in the third—each of which has involved a battle over the function of women's education and the content of the curriculum. They each involve separatism and considerations of vocational purpose, as well as the ideas of marriage and motherhood. The first phase, in part because it's the earliest, is the most persistent—and also the most acceptable to men. For these reasons, it is still a force today.

The women who fought the first series of battles for women's higher education in the early nineteenth century were interested in training teachers. They thought women should be educated separately from men, and for one specific vocational purpose: teaching. Three-quarters of the history of women's education in the nineteenth century—whether at single-sex or at allegedly coeducational institutions—is also the story of teacher education. We should all know these names: Mary Lyon, the founder in 1837 of Mt. Holyoke, Emma Willard, the founder in 1821 of Troy Seminary, Catherine Beecher, the founder of Hartford Seminary, and later of other schools for women in the midwest. They and others worked through the early decades of the nineteenth century to persuade men of the value of educating their daughters, and to raise funds for the establishment of permanent institutions for women. Abbott Female Academy, for example, was founded in Andover in 1829 for "young ladies who may wish to qualify themselves to teach."[5] Mary Lyon's "original and primary objective," as she worked through the 1830s to raise funds for opening Mt. Holyoke Seminary, "was the preparation of teachers for the millions crying for education, especially in the great valley of the West."[6] Mary Lyon's scheme was the education of very young women—admission to Mt. Holyoke at fourteen was not unusual—who would teach two to four years "and then marry," as she put it, "and become firm pillars to hold up their successors." What she called a "circulatory system" we would call a "revolving door." She firmly believed, however, that her scheme "would accomplish more for education than a smaller number of teachers who, by not marrying, could devote twenty or thirty years to the profession."[7] So teaching was not only an appropriate profession for women, it was also work that would prepare them for marriage, child-rearing, and the community support of education. In my archival research, I have found person after person, female and male, commenting or arguing that the education of women would not be wasteful, since, even if women married and therefore had to resign from their teaching jobs, their preparation was also useful for their expected work as mothers. Such statements, appearing either in catalogues themselves, or in presidents' reports, justify to a Board of Regents or to a legislature or to parents the expense involved in educating women, who, it was expected, would work for only a short period before marriage and motherhood.[8] Early feminists, too, regarded teaching as the prime means of earning a modest livelihood in dignified and socially useful work—for those women who could not or would not marry.

DEVELOPING A DIFFERENTNESS: FEMINISM'S FIRST PHASE

The feminist ideology behind such views of women's education emphasizes women's separate and subordinate social role. Women *are* different from men, such feminists proclaimed, but women ought to be allowed to develop that differentness for the greater good of society. As Emma Willard put it, schools for women ought to be "as different from those appropriated to the other sex, as the female character and duties are from the male." The purpose of such education is twofold: "implanting proper ideas and ideals in future mothers" and "furnishing properly trained teachers." The ultimate purpose is gloriously ideal: "to elevate the standards of morality and of public education."[9] The ideological portrait is incomplete, however, until we add Catherine Beecher's belief in the value of self-sacrifice. All of these women were devout Christians. For them, teaching was an appropriate female activity, since it was the obverse, secular version of clerical work. Women teachers were the secular arm of the church. Teachers were missionaries, moral emissaries, shapers of young minds and destinies. The purpose of women's education, according to Catherine Beecher, was to enable women "not to *shine,* but to *act.*"[10] And to *act,* of course, in a moral manner for its own sake, as a natural role model for others, and also as a deliberate modeler of others' morality. Catherine Beecher believed that women were especially suited for the role of moral teacher, since they were (a) "continually striving after purity" and (b) "consistently" self-sacrificial in their own homes (as contrasted with man's domestic selfishness and generosity outside the home).[11] The key ideas for this entire generation of feminist educators were sacrifice and service. Women, they argued, were better equipped than men for sacrifice and service. Mary Lyon described for her students the "opportunity for sacrificial service by 'going to destitute places in the West to labor' [meaning to teach in Ohio and Kansas]. As to pecuniary rewards, [she said] 'ladies sh'd not expect more than a mediocrity—less than $100 a year usually.'"[12]

Not surprisingly, a significant number of men including some in charge of education decided that it was in their interest to heed the pleas of these feminists. All the members of the Boards of Trustees and many of the financial supporters of early seminaries and later women's colleges and normal schools were men. And why not? These feminists were not challenging the status quo; they were simply saying we can do the child-rearing job better than men and even, on a massive scale, more economically. Not only are we women naturally more moral and thus more ready to maintain law and order; we are also self-sacrificing and thus we will do all this for the benefit of society and not our own pocketbooks. What has been called "the feminization of the teaching force"[13] satisfied both the nineteenth century's social need for an economical and efficient system of public education and the early feminists' need for work that could be rationalized without social offense.

Later in the century, with the extension of secondary education, and the growth of public education into large systems, once again the twin needs for "economy and improvement" extended the demand for women teachers. A School Committee in Quincy, Massachusetts in 1874, called for the establishment of large schools of 500 students, in which "one *man* (italics added) could be placed in charge. . . . Under his direction could be placed a number of female assistants." Females, the male Committee explained in 1874, "are not only adapted, but carefully trained, to fill such positions, as well [as] or better than men, excepting the master's place, which sometimes requires a man's force. . . ." And as if that were not enough reason—and of course ideologically from a male point of view it is not—the Committee added, "and the competition is so great [among women for these jobs and between women and men] that . . . [women's] services command less than one-half the wages of male teachers."[14]

On reflection, perhaps none of this history is surprising. How then does a subservient population convince its masters to allow it an increment of social progress? Obviously, by convincing the masters of its usefulness for *them*. Thus women teachers offered both an economical means to accomplish public education and the willingness as well to do so within the terms of the society's patriarchy. Women were to be taught how to teach the moral code that kept them enthralled in the first place. As Catherine Beecher put it, as early as 1829, "the most important object of education" is not the acquisition of knowledge, but, rather, "the formation of personal habits and manners, the correction of the disposition, the regulation of the social feelings, the formation of the conscience, and the direction of the moral character and habits." These, she said, "united, [are] objects of much greater consequence than the mere communication of knowledge and the discipline of the intellectual powers."[15]

If the function of such teaching was ultimately moral uplift for the nation, the curriculum had to reflect this goal. Teachers were the secular arm of the church; women as teachers could accomplish the moral reformation of character, a duty that the church allowed only to males. The curriculum that followed from such educational principles and goals supported patriarchy, and taught women that the home or, temporarily, the classroom was their appropriate domain. Catherine Beecher proposed a department of moral philosophy as the center of her school that would teach such principles to future teachers.

The curriculum differed in kind and degree from the classical education offered to their brothers through most of the 19th century; it simply verified women's distinct, traditional roles as nurturant servers of domestic life, propagators, child-rearers, and teachers. Women had to learn enough mathematics, and later science, as well as other skills to enable them to be adequate teachers of young children and older adolescents, but their education was not meant to develop in them the capacity either to question knowledge or to investigate its outer reefs. They learned enough to teach rudiments to others, not to shape knowledge anew.

But education, as we know, is not entirely predictable, or controllable. We often do not teach students what we want to or what we think we are teaching. The relationship between the early feminist educators I have been describing and the later ones connected to the founding of women's colleges after 1870 has not yet been traced in detail. The differences between the two groups concern us here, since we are the inheritors of their battle, the second major educational battle for women's education. That battle was initiated by the feminists we know as suffragists.

THE DRIVE FOR EQUALITY: FEMINISM'S SECOND PHASE

Both Elizabeth Cady Stanton (who went to Emma Willard's Troy Seminary) and Susan B. Anthony (who was of course a teacher) believed that there were no intellectual differences between men and women and that therefore their education ought to be identical, just as their social, economic, and political rights ought to be identical. Their ideology insisted on equality, not on distinct and separate spheres. And the founders of such colleges as Smith and Wellesley, as well as the second president of Bryn Mawr, M. Carey Thomas, put this theory into practice by adopting for women's colleges a curriculum identical to that prescribed for the men of Harvard and Yale. Women, such educators announced, could and should do all that men do.

So long as Latin and Greek were staples of that curriculum, women at Bryn Mawr or Smith did Latin and Greek. As the curriculum broadened at Harvard and much later at Yale, so did it at the elite women's colleges.

Here is M. Carey Thomas in 1901, arguing that the education of women must be no different from the education of men. "The burden of proof," she announces, "is with those who believe that the college education of men and women should differ."[16] She too focuses on vocation, but it is that of the professions themselves. Her argument rests on the assumption that "women are to compete with men" in those professions: "There is no reason to believe that typhoid or scarlet fever or phthsis can be successfully treated by a woman physician in one way and by a man physician in another way. There is indeed every reason to believe that unless treated in the best way the patient may die, the sex of the doctor affecting the result less even than the sex of the patient."[17] She argues similarly for bridge-building. And for cooking. And she concludes on a high note of warm optimism: "This college education should be the same as men's, not only because there is, I believe, but one best education, but because men and women are to live and work together as comrades and dear friends and married friends and lovers, and because their effectiveness and happiness and the welfare of the generation to come after them will be vastly increased if their college education has given them the same intellectual training and the same scholarly and moral ideals."[18]

But what, you may be wondering, of the coeducational colleges and universities, the Oberlin of 1837 and the land grant colleges after the Morrill Act of 1862? At Oberlin, the story is not an heroic one. Jill Conway, Smith College's new president, tells it in a recent essay in *Daedalus*: Oberlin was a "manual-work school" aimed to fill "an ever-expanding need [in the West] for trained clergy."

> In its early informal manifestations young men would undertake to work the land of a minister with sound theological knowledge if he would instruct them in return for their labor. Oberlin was a formal institutionalization of such an arrangement since the college was linked to a five hundred-acre farm where it was hoped that the students would produce enough in crops to reduce the cost of their education considerably. No sooner was the experiment launched, however, than it became clear that another element of cost could be eliminated if there were women students who could carry out the domestic chores in return for instruction. Once admitted to the college, they duplicated there all the existing service roles of women within the domestic economy. Classes were not held on Mondays so that the women students could launder and repair the men's clothes. Cooking and cleaning were done on a careful schedule outside classroom hours, and the women students always waited on table. Thus, the effect of the experiment was hardly consciousness-raising, and those few feminists, like Lucy Stone, who were early Oberlin graduates were radicals on such questions before they entered college.[19]

Women were offered a secondary curriculum, called "literary," and when one young woman in the first class wanted to study theology, she was not encouraged. Antoinette Brown, a close friend of Lucy Stone, attended classes in theology for an extra three years, though she was sometimes not allowed to participate in discussion; and indeed, she was not ordained there or graduated.[20]

Kansas State Agricultural College, now Kansas State University, one of the first of the land-grant colleges to be founded after the Morrill Act was passed, was a pioneer in practical education for an increasingly broad base of U.S. citizenry. Thus, in 1874, President John A. Anderson issued a *Hand-Book of the Kansas State Agricultural College* arguing the uselessness of a classical education in Latin, Greek, and Mathematics—a daring departure—and calling for the establishment of three curricula: 1) agricultural (only for men); 2) mechanics (engineering) (only for men); and 3) women's. The women's curriculum, an early version of home economics, provides for classes in "Special Hygiene" appropriate to women, "Gardening" (mainly ornamental without the "manual labor that should be done by men"); "Household Economy" (including "Lectures upon household chemistry . . . embracing cooking, domestic management, and kindred topics"); "Sewing"; and "Farm Economy" (including those operations which usually come under the supervision of the farmer's wife or daughter, and which are not included in "Gardening" or "Household Economy," such as butter and cheese making), as well as literature and other subjects appropriate to women. Kansas also pioneered courses in industrial arts, but these were also carefully sex-typed: printing, for example, in its English origins a woman's industry, was, in the 1874 curriculum, labeled as being only for men. (It was delightful to find it open to both sexes by the President who followed in 1880.) At other coeducational universities—I have worked in the archives, for example, of the University of Utah recently—it is clear that women were channelled into the Normal course—teacher education—and not into Mining and Metallurgy or Chemistry or other areas of hard science, law, or medicine.

And so there were two possibilities for women at coeducational institutions—and these are still possible today: first, women might study alongside men in such courses as U.S. history or the literature of Great Britain or introduction to psychology; in each case, the curriculum is designed for and geared to the interests and achievements of men—it is, as M. Carey Thomas so appropriately labeled it, the "men's curriculum."[21] Second, they might "elect" to study in almost totally female ghettoes—elementary education, for example, or home economics, or nursing. In these courses, the curriculum is for the most part still either male-centered, or male-biased. That is, women studying home economics assume that the traditional patriarchal forms of marriage and family organization are desirable, inevitable and unchangeable.

CHALLENGING MALE HEGEMONY: FEMINISM'S THIRD PHASE

By the early twentieth century, the impression is overwhelming that the education of women in women's colleges or in coeducational institutions continues to alternate between two poles: (1) that women need a separate, special education, for vocations especially suited to them—teaching, nursing, or social work, for example; and (2) that women are men's intellectual equals and may therefore appropriately study all that men do. In both cases women had to accept the traditional view of themselves as entering acceptable female-typed activities or professions; or taking the more daring position of M. Carey Thomas—that women were as good as men and therefore could do *men's* work. In neither case, however, had there been a challenge to male hegemony *over the curriculum or knowledge in general.* In neither case had women said, *no,* we are going to redefine the terms of the work world. We are going to look closely at the history of work and reassess job classifications in the rational light of social needs today. That is the crux for us today. In the past women either carved out for themselves an area that men didn't want anyway—domestic science, for example—or they studied within the purview of patriarchal knowledge, that is, history as males have seen it or known it, or science, with priorities established by males.

David Reisman, writing an introduction in 1964 to Jessie Bernard's *Academic Women,* conveniently summarizes the state of higher education for women with particular relevance for teacher education: "women," he says, "prefer to be *teachers, passing on a received heritage* and responsively concerning themselves with their students, while men of equivalent or even lesser ability prefer to be *men-of-knowledge, breaking the accustomed mold* and remaining responsive not to students but to the structure of the discipline and their colleagues in the invisible university (italics added)."[22]

Just one decade later, this sentence sharply divides the past from the present. Yes, I say reading it, that was the way it was for 150 years. Now it's different. Women will no longer be content to pass on "a received heritage"; rather, women have become, are becoming, in Reisman's terms, women-of-knowledge, "breaking the accustomed mold."

I am of course referring to women's studies which as far as I can see historically is truly a new, third feminist development. For the first time, feminists in an organized manner are querying education's ultimate—the curriculum and the sources of that curriculum, knowledge itself. Unlike the work of earlier feminists like Catherine Beecher, moreover, the queries are not confined to women's domestic sphere, but encompass many of the traditional male bastions, especially history, economics, sociology, psychology, anthropology, law, even medicine, as well as literature and the arts. Indeed, without the perspective provided by what we call women's studies, I couldn't have traced the preceding historical patterns, and I would not be here today.

The new feminism is profoundly different from both forms of the old. We are saying today not simply allow us a piece of the turf (Beecher, Lyon, and others of the first wave), or let us into your castle (second wave: equality) but rather, let us reexamine the whole question, all the questions. Let us take nothing for granted. Most definitely, let us refuse to pass on that "received heritage" without examining its cultural bias. And since women are half the population, they are black as well as white, poor as well as rich, they include all religions, all national and ethnic origins; since one can't talk about women as a monolith, examining cultural bias becomes a complex task far-reaching in its potential for education.

Let me give you one immediate and practical example of current feminist thought about the curriculum. The study of American literature is not as old as the history I have been describing. The formal study of both English and U.S. literature hearkens back less than 100 years. A staple of such reading has been Benjamin Franklin's *Autobiography*. Why? Why have millions of us, female and male, members of minorities and whites, rich and poor, been handed Franklin and not Frederick Douglass, for example, or Elizabeth Cady Stanton? (I won't detour into questions of literary style, but both Douglass and Stanton are at least as interesting on that count as Franklin.) New feminists are not saying that Franklin ought to be dismissed, but they question his value as a single representative of *all* Americans. They are saying that the life of one white male is inadequate to represent us all: his life needs to be viewed in the company of at least one woman's life; moreover, white lives are, alone, inadequate: they ought to be viewed in the company of at least the lives of some members of minorities.

This is a very different kind of feminism from Beecher's or Thomas'. Beecher might have wished her students to study women's lives, but not Stanton's, for she was a rebel. Beecher thought that women teachers should learn their subordinate role exceedingly well. She did not think women ought to get into politics; their domain was the household and, temporarily, the classroom. M. Carey Thomas would also not have argued for reading Stanton's life; she wanted her students to be prepared exactly as men were. That meant follow the leader, read whatever men decided should be read.

New feminists like me are saying, let us look closely at this polyglot. Let us review the hierarchy. Let us study not one life as an example of how we were or how we ought to be. Let us study many lives—and what is equally important—how these lives related each to each. Why could Elizabeth Cady Stanton in 1830 not follow her brother to Union College? What college could a black person, male or female, attend in 1830? And how did educational deprivation affect her/his life and opportunities? More significantly, read in the company of Franklin's life, Stanton's tells us that bearing and rearing seven children did not prevent her from accomplishments that can be matched by few males in any century.

Today we inherit both sets of ideas about the education of women. Many of us still see women as more honest, virtuous, self-sacrificing, and hence more willing to serve—meaning teach—than men. Others see women as potentially as capable as men in all their spheres. Those who hold this view will usually adopt males as models for female accomplishment: you have heard women say, we can do anything men can do. Feminists today may be found in both those camps still, though I believe that the central thrust of today's feminists needs to be different. Especially for those engaged in education, feminism in all its forms is once again of central importance. On the one hand, we live in a sex-role defined job world. The ghettoes of nursing, elementary education, office work, and social work are realities. On the other hand, we are urging students to enter "nontraditional"—meaning male—fields.

And now I'd like to return to my original questions. Have I learned —am I learning—anything of immediate use for those of us engaged in women's studies? The answer is yes and no. Yes, it seems to me that for the first time I can see the logic of our feminist history and I can appreciate and understand those women who struggled for their modest goals. Without them, we could not now be insisting that we too have a history to study and learn from. Their achievements as well as their strategies and tactics are not inconsiderable and we have much to learn from them.

On the other hand, there is no clear model for the current development of women's studies. That is not difficult to understand. It means that we have not been, before today, convinced of our own hegemony over knowledge, our own power to decide about the curriculum. That is an awesome responsibility. We do not want Harvard as a model. We know its severe limitations. We do not have elder brothers, male patrons to establish institutions and guidelines for us. Remember, it was Henry Durant, the intrepid founder of Wellesley, who not only said "Women can do the work. I give them the chance"—but also who made it possible.[23] Today, we are making it possible, and the revision of the curriculum, the explosion of knowledge in all fields, will affect men as well as women. Ultimately— perhaps I am describing still another century of struggle—we will live in a very different educational world.

So, you have heard my optimism, and I am sometimes attacked for it, especially by academics who are "naturally" cynical. Reading history has made me more rather than less optimistic. In 1938, when Virginia Woolf wrote a militant feminist and pacifist book called *Three Guineas,* she asked the key question that new feminists have been asking these past 10 years. She looked at "our brothers who have been educated at public schools and universities" and asked other women, "Do we wish to join that procession, or don't we? On what terms shall we join that procession? Above all, where is it leading us, the procession of educated men?"[24] Virginia Woolf concluded, as you know, that the procession was leading us downhill to war and to the degeneration of the human race. Yet she saw no way out for sisters but to join the procession, even on its own terms, for women then were powerless—without education, jobs, professions, money.

If I am optimistic today, it is because I think that a sizable number of us with and without jobs, professions, money, are prepared, have begun, to turn the procession at least half an inch off course. Another way to put it is to say that because of the history I have outlined, because of the positions and concessions of earlier feminists, we are more numerous and more powerful today. I am optimistic that we will use that power ultimately and well.

Spring 1975

[1] During the academic year 1974-75, I worked in college and university archives under a Ford Foundation Fellowship for the Study of Women in Society. I am obliged especially to Mariam Chamberlain for her vision and support of my work in the history of women's education.

[2] Patsy Schweickert is identified only as being "at Ohio State University." The essay appeared in *The University of Michigan Papers in Women's Studies*, vol. 1, no. 3, October 1974, pp. 147–157.

[3] See, for example, *Feminist Resources for Schools and Colleges,* now being revised for its Second Edition by Merle Froschl and Jane Williamson. (Old Westbury, New York: The Feminist Press, 1976).

[4] The information here is based on *Who's Who and Where in Women's Studies* (Old Westbury, New York: The Feminist Press, 1974). By 1976, the numbers are quite different. There are more than two hundred women's studies programs—and no way to count the thousands of courses.

[5] Arthur C. Cole, *A Hundred Years of Mount Holyoke College* (New Haven, Yale University Press, 1940), p. 9.

[6] *Ibid.,* p. 120.

[7] *Ibid.,* p. 123.

[8] Men, it should be remembered, were not forced to resign upon marriage. It was not until the nineteen-thirties that women teachers began to gain the right—through unionization—to work after marriage.

[9] Cole, pp. 4–5.

[10] Kathryn Kish Sklar, *Catherine Beecher: A Study in American Domesticity* (New Haven: Yale University Press, 1973), p. 76.

[11] *Ibid.,* p. 86.

[12] Cole, p. 122.

[13] Michael B. Katz, "The 'New Departure' in Quincy, 1873–81: The Nature of Nineteenth-Century Educational Reform," *Education in American History: Readings on the Social Issues,* ed. Michael B. Katz (New York: Praeger, 1973), p. 73.

[14] *Ibid.*

[15] Sklar, p. 91.

[16] M. Carey Thomas, "Education for Women and for Men," *The Educated Woman in America,* ed. Barbara M. Cross (New York: Teachers College Press, 1965), p. 152.

[17] *Ibid.,* p. 147.

[18] *Ibid.,* p. 154.

[19] Jill Conway, "Coeducation and Women's Studies: Two Approaches to the Question of Woman's Place in the Contemporary University," *Daedalus,* Fall 1974, p. 242.

[20] I appreciate use of a chapter on Antoinette Brown's life at Oberlin, soon to appear in a new biography by Elizabeth Cazden to be published in 1977 by The Feminist Press.

[21] Thomas, in Cross, p. 153.

[22] David Riesman, "Introduction" to Jessie Bernard's *Academic Women* (New York: New American Library, 1964), p. xvii.

[23] Alice Hackett Harter, *Wellesley: Part of the American Story* (Lexington, Mass.: Stone Wall Press, Inc., 1949), p. 38.

[24] Virginia Woolf, *Three Guineas* (London, The Hogarth Press, 1952), pp. 110, 113.